The BunkerBook

Nuggets of Liberty From The Freedom Bunker

By Chris Future

freedombunker.com

My name is Chris Future, and I've produced both a audio podcast (900+ episodes) and a YouTube video channel (300+ episode) over the last 6 years, featuring news, politics and libertarian rants, and not necessarily those, and not necessarily in that order. But I digress!

Over the course of my journey into the wide world of podcasting, video blogging and blogging, I've come across a bunch of truisms that helped me form my political beliefs, helped me through life, and sometimes made me laugh. This book is a compendium of a few of those things.

There is one consistent theme that I kept coming across over and over again in my travels, and that theme was that, to some degree, no matter where they are on the political spectrum, unless of course they are totalitarian dictators or narcissistic Marxists, underlying most people's political beliefs is a libertarian foundation.

Some of us have embraced it, others deny it, but by the end of this book, I hope to prove to you that yes, to some degree, YOU are a libertarian, and that it's just fine to come out and say it.

My hope is that by the end of this book, you'll close it up, think deeply and say to yourself (or out loud if you are alone – I suppose you could do it out loud when you are around others but they may elicit some funny looks), I AM A LIBERTARIAN. At least to some degree.

I believe that, on some level, as Americans, even as human, we have always been libertarians. It just got obscured by all of this left v right nonsense.

So go forth, and be free.

Not a Lecture

Like I always say on my show, this is not a lecture, it's a conversation, so please feel free to contact me, I love connecting with people and discussing important issues: we may not always agree, but at least we are still allowed to speak:

- Email: thinkfuture@gmail.com
- IM: thinkfuture, on Yahoo! Instant Messenger
- Site: http://freedombunker.com
- Twitter: http://twitter.com/bunkerblast
- Facebook: http://facebook.com/chrisfutureshow

Hope to hear from you soon!

Table Of Contents

You Are Probably A Libertarian and Don't Even Know It.

- Do you believe in social freedoms?
- Do you believe that people should be left alone to live their lives, as long as it doesn't hurt anyone?
- Do you believe in fiscal responsibility?
- Do you believe that you should be allowed to keep as much of your income as possible?
- Do you believe in lower taxes?
- Do you believe that the state is doing too much?

Then you are probably a libertarian and don't even know it. You know, there are tons of people out there who seem lost. They look at both the Republicans and Democrats and say to themselves, well gee, I agree with this side on that issue and with the other side on the other issue. But I can't really bring myself to buying into the whole thing: you are into not spending your money on people, who can't fend for themselves, but you also aren't interested in telling people how to live their lives; but neither party lets you think that.

Or you read up on Ron Paul and thought – yes, he had the right idea, but you've been a lifelong Democrat, or maybe you thought there was no way he could win, but you thought: you know what, of all of them, he was the most right.

Well, my friend, then you probably are a libertarian and don't even know it.

Welcome.

Trust me. This is the right decision. Both parties have strayed far too far from our founding principles. This is the only option left to you now.

Be proud to be a libertarian. Pull up a chair, take off your coat, and stay awhile.

I think you'll like it.

Social Freedom, Fiscal Responsibility, Limited Government

See, it's not hard to figure it out once you think about it and break out of your two party rut.

For example, Democrats usually champion human rights and free speech. Although, of late, under Obama's administration, they seem to be doing the opposite. And the Republicans usually champion fiscal responsibility. Although of late, under the Bush Administration, and actually most administrations since Reagan's, they seem to be doing the opposite.

So what is a person to do? Make a choice which sacrifices one for the other? What if you want both social freedoms AND fiscal responsibility? Is it some kind of two-headed monster, ala The Thing with Two Heads? (Actually, we'll talk about racism later.) Not really. It's a libertarian viewpoint. Although both Democrats and Republicans do treat us as such. They say: oh my, look at those lunatics, thinking for themselves. They both know that's bad, that's why they don't encourage it.

Plus, we are for limited government. We want to limit the states intervention in our lives. When was the last time any administration did that, left or right, Republican or Democrat? Not since before Roosevelt, eh? (BTW: if you see me use "eh?" instead of "huh?" at the end of some sentences, that would be my Canadian roots showing). Both the Republicans and the Democrats expanded the size of the state in the last two administrations more than ever before, the (R)s did it in the name of security, and the (D)s did it in the name of social programs, but in the end it's the same: more debt than ever before. A debt which we and our children will have to pay for for generations to come.

The only way forward is less government, not more.

The people need to be back in charge.

Be Independent

You know what separates us from the rest of the animal kingdom? Do you know what makes us different from every other animal out there?

Those of you who believe that the human race is a blight on the world, you'll say something like "Man is the only creature that kills each other" or some such nonsense. Or that "we subjugate every other creature" blah blah blah. Well that one is almost right.

There is one thing we have that no other species on this planet has.

Give up?

It's our capacity to **THINK**. It's the ability to **REASON**.

It's our brain. Our ability to think and reason separates us from all of the other creatures on this planet.

So you wonder, gee, if we have this great capacity to think, how come so few of us actually do? Present company excepted, of course, since you bought and are reading this book.

When I turn on the TV and I see millions of people in tears based on the words of some politician from Chicago installed into the presidency, or some talk show host opining about relationships followed by millions, or some celebrity urging people to dig deep for some pet cause, and people following like herds of sheep, what is there to think?

Why do so many of us take our innate ability to think and reason, check it out of our heads, put it on a shelf, and walk in lockstep with all of these other "sheep"? Why do we take our "special sauce", the thing that makes us human, and disregard it thus?

Sure, it's hard to be human. It's difficult to go through life always thinking about things. It's just so much easier to just give up, take out that ability, put it on a shelf, and just follow the herd.

Don't you understand? When you do that, you are not being human anymore! You literally have a choice, every second of every day, to be human, or to be animal. When you use your ability to think and reason, you are human, when you don't you are animal.

You are a thinking human being with a capacity for reason. Use that brain. Don't walk in lockstep with everyone else.

Personal Responsibility

I drove past a great billboard the other day: it was an ad for the San Francisco 49ers. There was a giant photo of some player, in full regalia, helmet, uniform, hand outstretched as if to reach for something. Sure it was an ad for a sports team, but it was a powerful statement in general. In very large type, it read:

"NO ONE GIVES YOU ANYTHING, YOU HAVE TO TAKE IT."

I thought wow, what a close analogy to life. I'd modify it slightly of course to read:

"NO ONE GIVES YOU ANYTHING, YOU HAVE TO EARN IT."

For too long, we have set up systems which interconnect us, via the state, which take too much and give too little. They have completely ignored the simple statement above. That is what life is. Nothing IS given to you, or should be given to you. One needs to earn it. Deep down, even the most liberal believe in this: it's an innate human thing, the struggle to survive is deep in our genes, no matter how we try to suppress it, it's there and will always be there.

It starts with the state. It extends to the parents who don't properly raise their children, instead churning out dependent humans who cannot get through life on their own. And that's wrong. The job of a parent is to create a fully fleshed out human being, who can make their own decisions, take full responsibility for their lives and their futures.

Like Ayn Rand said "I swear, by my life and my love of it, that I will never live for the sake of another man, nor ask another man to live for mine." We should ask or expect anyone to live for anyone's sake but their own, and if they choose to, their families.

Remember the election, when some of Obama's supporters were calling for his election because "Obama would pay for my gas and mortgage"?

When did we go from a culture of independence to a culture of dependence?

The reality is simple. No one is responsible for anyone other than themselves, unless they choose to take on the burden of others. No one should be forced to take on another's burden. But we are forced to do that every day, when we pay out millions upon millions of dollars in taxes in order to support the "less well off"

Well, I'm calling for a return to the days of personal responsibility. No longer are criminals the result of the culture that they grew up in, but people who made choices.

We all make our own beds, and we all should sleep in them.

This doesn't mean that we stop freely giving to those we deem less fortunate. If you or I saw someone that we wanted to help and support, no matter the cause, we should be able to.

What I'm railing against is the state using our money for causes which don't align with our world view. For example, would an anti-abortionist agree with their tax dollars supporting an abortion clinic?

Would a atheist agree with their tax dollars going to faith-based initiatives? When government takes money out of our hands and spends it on our behalf for causes we disagree with, that's wrong, and you have to agree with that – no matter which side of the political spectrum you are on.

DIY Moral Code

Why does it have to be all or nothing? When you hook up with any major religion, they usually have a big list of do's and don'ts right? Like, for example, let's take a look my rough translation of the Ten Commandments. Now, now, I'm not being overly Christian here, fact is most religions and philosophies have a top ten "this is how to behave list". In philosophy we call it Ethics, or 'moral philosophy', which is concerned with questions of how persons ought to act or if such questions are answerable. Course you knew that:

1. I'm the boss, and don't you forget it
2. Nobody else is the boss, just me - you are not the boss.
3. Don't talk about me
4. Take at least one day off every week to rest up and tell me how wonderful I am
5. Make sure that you are nice to your Mom & Dad. If it weren't for them, you wouldn't exist
6. Don't kill anybody
7. Don't sleep around on your significant other
8. Don't steal stuff
9. Don't lie about other people
10. Don't envy what other people have

Of course they stop here, since after this they start talking about drilling holes in ears using augurs, slaves and fence posts, so I guess someone figured out that maybe just a top ten would suffice.

First of all, those first 4 won't work for me. I don't think anyone else should be telling me what to do right? Five is OK, but only if your parents raised you to be an independent thinking person, which you probably are since you bought this book. Six also seems reasonable, I mean unless someone wants to kill you first. Seven is really a breach of contract, so also reasonable. Eight seems OK too, since like 6, I don't want anyone killing me either. Nine is pretty good as well, since again, I'd prefer people wouldn't lie about me. And 10 is a bit of a crock, I mean, if I didn't envy what other people have, where's my ambition to strive for more? Gone!

So, I'll toss 1-4 and 10, and keep 5-9. So I follow the 5 commandments. And maybe add a few more of my own. Like "do the right thing", "follow up" and "finish what you start".

Why not? Who says we have to follow all this stuff in lockstep? As thinking, rational human beings, the only thing we have that separates us from the animals is our capacity to think. To REASON.

Embrace Change

You know what's interesting? There is a simple fact of life many people don't get. But as an added bonus for buying this book, I'm going to reveal this super-secret secret of life. I know, I know, once you read it you'll go, of course duh. But let me tell you first and then explain why people don't believe it after.

Here is the fact:

LIFE IS CHANGE

There, I said it. You are saying, duh. Everyone knows that. But do you? Do you really? And if you know that, then why are you surprised by anything? Once you truly get it, and understand that life is change, then trust me, things will get better.

Why you ask?

I'll tell you. If you truly believe that life is change, then nothing will surprise you. Everything that crosses your path which throws you off, won't. And if something still does throw you off, then you know that you really still don't believe in the above.

But even if you go so far as to say, sure I believe in the above, and are not surprised, still you worry. You worry about losing your job, your home, your spouse, your life, gaining a new job, buying a new house, having a baby, and any and all of the myriad things that will happen in your life. Some will be good and some will be bad. The fact is that whether its good or bad, it's still change.

So how do you deal with all of the change in life, good or bad? Simple. Don't just deal with change as it comes:

EMBRACE IT

If you embrace change when it comes, and you know it will, you can truly have a fulfilling, calm and wonderful life. And how do you embrace change? Also simple:

Do. Fail. Learn. Do again until you succeed.

Pretty simple, huh? I see people make up all these elaborate plans, and then something in life comes along and changes everything, and then they have to write up whole new plans and everything. So why do it? If life is change, how much planning can you really do? Plan your work and work your plan, may be great for some things, but it doesn't work for life.

Don't be afraid to fail.

Every failure is an opportunity to learn.

Wealth = Work

What's with all the hate on for rich people nowadays? I mean you'd think that these people were rich because they stole all that money from people. What are rich people nowadays? I mean, let's take a quick look at those folks at the top of the Forbes 400 and let's see how they got rich:

1. William Gates III: computer software people buy for their computers
2. Warren Buffett: people buy places to live, stay and house their businesses from this guy
3. Lawrence Ellison: more computer software people buy for their computers
4. Christy Walton: people buy stuff at her store
5. Jim C. Walton: OK, I guess it's his store too
6. Alice Walton: and hers!
7. S. Robson Walton: and his! Man, Sam had a lot of kids.
8. Michael Bloomberg: people pay for his info and buy his newspapers and stuff
9. Charles Koch: people buy stuff he makes, like petroleum, paper towels, fertilizer and fibers etc.
10. David Koch : I guess he's in on it with his bro, Chuck.

I'm pretty sure that the Google guys, the Dell guy, and a whole bunch of others are right in there as well. What's the deal with these folks? I mean, as far as I can tell, unless overcharging for a crappy product is theft, (apologies Bill, but Windows 7 is OK), none of these people are stealing your money. They provide a useful product or service in exchange for your hard earned money.

This is not the middle ages. We are no longer in the land of kings and queens and landed gentry, where there was a rich ruling class which was rich because they stole from the poor. The rich of today are rich because people pay them for something that they have created and they believe has value.

They didn't steal from us. They are rich because we gave them our money willingly in exchange for things like Xbox 360s, the apartment we live in, or groceries. Why should we steal from them, via the state increasing taxes by huge amounts in the name of fairness?

Yes, Bill Gates is probably richer than you. But remember, Bill Gates creates something you usually are willing to pay for that gives you value. And he employs many people. Whole industries are built on what he has created. So why should we hate him? We should laud him for all the good work he has done, and encourage him to do more.

The rich of today are the ones we should be saluting, not the politicians of today, who only seem to be able to tear down, not build up. Who is the better man? The man who creates wealth and jobs, or the man who steals wealth and destroys jobs?

I think you know the answer.

Garbage = Power

I am firmly convinced that the only reason people go into government is to control others. Let me tell you a little story.

I used to live in an area where our trash pickup was on Wednesdays. When I moved into that area, we got a letter from the trash company saying to put out the trash the night before, since the trash pickup could come anytime between 6am and 3pm, depending on how busy the "sanitation engineers" were that day. So I did so.

Eventually, I noted that every Wednesday, without fail, for more than a year, the truck would come by after 10am, in fact sometimes as late as 5pm, but always, always after 10am. Every Wednesday, like clockwork, after 10am.

So eventually, I, and everyone else on the street, got used to taking out the trash on Wednesday morning, trusting that by the evidence piled up over the last year, that the truck would not be by until after most of us had left for work.

So that's what we all did. Every Wednesday morning, we'd greet each other on our way to take out the trash bins and get in our cars and go. This went on for over a year.

Then one day, I'm lying in bed. It's 6am Wednesday morning. I just woke up. And what do I hear?

Yes, folks. It's the garbage truck, banging, slamming and grinding and grunting.

So I jump up – hurriedly put on some clothes and tear out the door, half asleep, pulling my bins to the curb in the ungodly early early very cold morning. As were almost all of my neighbors, in various stages of dress. Some of us just didn't make it in time. We grumbled and went back to bed.

So maybe after I thought, OK, maybe they changed their shift. So we all started dutifully putting our bins out the night before. Guess what?

They started coming after 10am again. And as far as I know, they are still coming after 10am.

This is what I think happened: Some government functionary in the always interesting waste removal division was incredibly bored one day, or had a fight with his wife, or was constipated, or was pissed off because he didn't get a promotion, whatever. This guy decided, simply because he can, to screw with our heads. He probably called the waste removal company and changed the schedule on purpose just to screw us all over. I'm sure that he got a great laugh about it.

So this is my theory. Why does anyone get into government? Why would anyone aspire to be a "public servant" (chuckle), unless it was to run other people's lives? Cause if you ask me, anyone who doesn't want to run other people's lives should just get into the business world. That's where you can't survive simply telling people what to do.

Planning vs. Resilience

If life is change, then how does planning work?

I firmly believe that there are two core ways in which to run your life. You can either:

- Plan everything out to the Nth degree, and hope nothing upsets your plan
- Expect that something will happen to ruin what you are doing, and be able to bounce back

A lot of people believe in the "plan it all out" strategy. Problem is that life does not work that way. Life is change, and no matter how you plan, invariably something will happen that you cannot plan for. And in that case, all of your planning will be for nothing.

I read this great article in a now defunct magazine which was part of the Forbes empire – it was called Forbes ASAP, and it was all about leading tech thought and investment etc. The article was called "How the West Kicked Butt" – I'm sure that if you Google it or something you'll find it.

Anyways, in this article, the author postulated that the reason the west coast was getting tons more investment than the east coast was the "style" of the place as opposed to the ideas coming out of that place. The author suggested that the difference was planning vs resilience – and used the weather and earthquakes as the metaphor. On the east coast, you know that during the upcoming winter, you are probably in for terrible weather. So you prepare for the weather: you buy warm clothes, you get snow tires for your car etc. You have some idea what is going to happen so you plan your life. So planning is a big deal. The better your plan, the better you can deal with this known quantity: bad weather. On the west coast, on the other hand, you have no idea when a devastating earthquake may occur.

So you can't plan for it: sure you can get supplies in etc in case one occurs, but you can't really plan for when it happens. So what is a big deal? Bouncing back from disaster: or resilience. The ability to claw back from bad things that happen. That's more important than planning on the west coast.

So why is resilience better than planning? Simple. This article was focused on business and investment: it supposed that venture investors would prefer to invest in companies which could survive sudden adverse conditions.

So I thought, life is like that too. Being able to survive sudden adverse conditions is much more critical to life than planning out your every step.

So to all of those people who plan out their lives to the Nth degree, I say:

RELAX. Sure, make a plan, but don't go overboard. Life will get in the way. That's its job. Instead, focus on being able to bounce back from adversity. Move on quickly.

Like in craps. When you throw a bad roll, you just move on to the next shooter. You don't sit there and focus on that guy who just lost you $1200.

Just move on to the next win.

Public vs. Private

Let me ask you something about the last time you went to a private company and the last time you had to deal with the state. I'll take a simple example and compare:

You go to Nordstrom's:

You walk in, and are greeted by the nearest sales person. They ask if you need any help and then let you browse. If you look lost, they help you find what you are looking for. Then they help you pick the product you wish to purchase. If you need to try things on, they bring things to you, and let you try them. They help you with your purchase as much as they can. And whether you buy something or not, they are always helpful and cheerful. You leave the store in an optimistic mood, whether you buy anything or not.

You go to the DMV:

You walk into the DMV and get a number. And wait. And wait. And wait. When your number is called, many minutes later, you are greeted by a surly clerk who brusquely tells you what you can and cannot do. They ask you to spend even more minutes completing paperwork asking you private questions that they have no business asking. After many more minutes, they take your paperwork. They then ask you to pay an exorbitant amount for a service that has no useful purpose to you. They give you more paperwork, and force you to pay for a service to "smog" your car at a third party private business. You eventually leave, much of your time wasted, your wallet empty, and feeling screwed over, and in a pessimistic mood.

Which do you prefer? Dealing with a private company that has a vested interest in keeping you happy, so that you will freely pay for a product or service from them? Or a public concern which doesn't care about your feelings, moods, preferences, and makes money by stealing from you, and providing no services which benefit you at all in any way shape or form.

Would you really prefer that the state provide you with healthcare? Of all of the things the state could provide, do you really think that it can be trusted with something as important as your life? I mean this about it for a second: why this headlong rush to giving the government more and more power in order to "fix" things, instead of taking power away from the government and letting the people fix things? I mean, what was the last thing that you can recall that the government actually "fixed" instead of "broke"?

Recently, in my area, there was a high school that was pretty bad – in fact so bad that they had to have a private security detail come in and stop some of the lawless behavior at the school. However, since the budget crisis hit, they had to cut the security force. Everyone was up in arms – oh my God they would say – the school will now become a war zone. What are we to do? But guess what: when the security guards left – when the authority figures split – it turns out that violence actually went down and the students started to police themselves. Peer pressure was a more powerful motivator than force. This is probably typical: take away the authority and people will self organize to make things better. It's a proven fact.

So take government away, and we can run things ourselves, a thousand times better.

Multiculturalism vs. Melting Pot

Do you know why America is better than every other country? It's pretty simple. America has a "melting pot" and most other countries are into "multiculturalism" What are the differences you ask?

Melting Pot: (from Wikipedia)

In the eighteenth and nineteenth century, the metaphor of a "crucible" or "(s)melting pot" was used to describe the fusion of different nationalities, ethnicities and cultures. It was used together with concepts of America as an ideal republic and a "city upon a hill" or new promised land. It was a metaphor for the idealized process of immigration and colonization by which different nationalities, cultures and "races" (a term that could encompass nationality, ethnicity and race) were to blend into a new, virtuous community, and it was connected to utopian visions of the emergence of an American "new man". The exact term "melting pot" came into general usage in 1908, after the premiere of the play the melting pot by Israel Zangwill.

Multiculturalism: (also from Wikipedia)

Multiculturalism is the acceptance of multiple ethnic cultures, for practical reasons and/or for the sake of diversity and applied to the demographic make-up of a specific place, usually at the organizational level, e.g. Schools, businesses, neighbourhoods, cities or nations. In this context, multiculturalists advocate extending equitable status to distinct ethnic and religious groups without promoting any specific ethnic, religious, and/or cultural community values as central.

What does this mean? Well, it means that when you come to America, you are expected to be American first, and then celebrate your other culture. Your "Americaness" should take priority over whatever else you are. So if you are from Greece originally, sure you can still maintain your Greek culture, but not are the expense of being American. You are American first, adopting the culture, laws and customs of America, and Greek second. The core of American culture thus progresses and is maintained by a strong connection to being American, life liberty, the pursuit of happiness and all that good stuff.

In multicultural societies, like Canada, the UK, most of Europe and many others, immigrants to these countries are allowed to maintain their culture as a higher priority than taking on the culture of the country they have adopted. These countries willingly allow their new immigrants and citizens to subsume their culture under the immigrant's culture, and in some cases, laws and customs. In the process, instead of the adopted countries culture being strengthened by the immigrant, as they add to the culture as a whole, they take from the culture. They weaken the culture. They, in some cases, actively work to take down and/or modify the culture of their adopted country. They try to get the best of both worlds, the services and opportunity of the new country, and the old rivalries and hatreds of the old country.

Progressives love the multicultural vision, thinking that it makes them so tolerant. But it comes at a huge cost to the culture of the adopted country. America has toyed with it, but make no mistake, if we adopt it, it will be the end of America. Now please understand, I'm not saying to completely divest yourself of your home countries culture when you emigrate to America. You can still of course honor the culture of your country in a million different ways, but since you came to this country most likely in order to avoid persecution and/or for the great economic opportunity America affords, you should honor America and its culture as well, don't you think?

We are already seeing some steps in that direction. When was the last time you saw a flyer from any branch of the government that only came in English?

But wait you say, Future, you are just being racist. Au contraire, I say. Asking someone to adapt to our culture is very different from accommodating every other culture above our own. We HAVE a very strong culture of our own, and most immigrants (at least the legal ones) are here so that they can benefit from the opportunities America affords them, not the services the American government provides via theft.

America is special for a reason. People come here looking for a better life, so why encourage them to have the same life in a different place?

Honor what we have built here, it's good. People emigrate to America more than any other country for a reason. Let's keep that reason solid.

Agreements

When two or more people agree to do something, we make agreements, verbal or otherwise. When we make these agreements, we should follow through with those agreements, unless one party of the other violates the spirit of the agreements. That is what is known as integrity:

1. You promise to do something
2. You do it.

What if you promise to do something, then don't do it? Or you promise to do something, but then do something else, without even asking the other party if it would be okay to do this other thing? Or just decide, for no reason whatsoever, to screw the other person, because you wanted to change the terms of the agreement to your own benefit.

Now that wouldn't be very nice would it? But the state does this, on a regular basis, with no moral qualms about it whatsoever. In fact, the state firmly believes that it can change any agreement, at will and with no justification. They are like the spoiled child who first wants one thing, then immediately the other, as long as THEY benefit. They do not care what you want.

When everything in the economy started to fall apart in the big crash of 2009-2010, the Obama administration went back and started re-writing contracts which were already written between employers and employees. They were going back and looking at how much money they employees were making and making decisions based on fairness.

Imagine how that might work:

1. You get a job
2. When you accept that job, both you and your employer decide on a fair salary for your work
3. You go on the assumption that for the work you are performing, you will be paid that salary
4. You expect your company to meet the agreement in paying you that salary, and you expect to fulfill your duties in order to provide service to your employer in exchange for that salary

Sounds good so far right? Typical job situation. Then the government gets involved.

1. The federal government decides that your company must be penalized for some reason. Usually because they have done their jobs too well and made money. Most governments penalize success.
2. The penalty has nothing to do with your personal performance at the company
3. Even so, it reviews your companies books and decides that someone in your position is overpaid for the work that you do
4. It goes back and "reassesses" your salary based on some new arbitrary number that it

feels you are worth, not an agreed upon amount which was determined based on market forces at the time you accepted the job.

5. It retroactively revises your contract, so that you are now at this new salary, which was NOT arrived at via an agreement between you and your employer

Some of you might think – that's not a big deal. Employers do this all the time. You just have to suck it up.

Big big difference, people. Employers do it in order to survive. Plus they work within the confines of the contract itself. They don't arbitrarily, retroactively change the terms of the agreements that they have with you.

What the government is saying is that any and all agreements, even those they don't enter into – can be rendered null and void, anytime they want them to. It's like there is no more rule of law.

If this is allowed to continue, America will be indistinguishable from the dictatorships we fight against.

Making the World Safe for Capitalism

Bush was partly right. Democracy is important. But I'd argue that if anything capitalism may even be more important.

You see, democracy is only half of the picture. Remember Bush's vaunted "War on tyranny" everywhere? This is yet another one of the marketing slogans he used, right alongside the "ownership society". So we are fighting this tyranny everywhere, but helping to overthrow these regimes and installing democracies. (Well, supposedly we were, until Obama came onto the scene). But installing democracy isn't enough, since it only goes so far.

These countries need a damn good dose of capitalism as well. It's a proven fact that nothing does a culture more good than a big dose of freedom and money which can be gained through work.

Democracy doesn't do anything about truly empowering people directly: all that it does it gives you the choice of selecting which tyrant will lord it over you – it gives no real power or influence to the people. You still only have a finite set of choices of "leader" – and most of the time, they are just out for themselves anyways. Remember Election 2008? Was there any real choice between the soft leftism of McCain and the hard leftism of Obama. Same thing, different name.

Capitalism truly gives the power back to the people. In a capitalistic society, the people create their own wealth, they don't expect it from an overarching government. They go out and make their own luck, their own money. It's the ultimate in personal responsibility.

Actually, I take back what I said at the top of this section: we don't really need democracy. We need democracy in order to implement capitalism: democracy lets us implement capitalism without fiat. Trust me, people want to be free. It's a proven fact.

If we could implement capitalism, then let the democracy flow from the freedom and trust and economic power that capitalism unleashes that might even work better.

Internet vs. Tyranny

The Internet will let people beat tyranny, not any the state. Basically, the state IS tyranny. They can't work without it.

Do you want to know why the Bush administration, Obama and the current Democratic administration want to put curbs on Internet speech? Do you know why China already has curbs on Internet speech? It's simple really.

The state does not want people talking to each other. And the internet is the ultimate peer-to-peer, or person-to-person communications mechanism. Its whole foundation is communications from any "node" to any other "node"

For the first time in human history, the Internet and the web provide a medium upon which every human being on the planet can talk to any other human being on the planet, be it via voice, text, and image whatever.

Think about it for a second: imagine a world where everyone on the planet has an iPhone, or iPhone like device, which gives them totally free, unfettered access to READ about anything and everything which is happening everywhere else. Can you imagine what someone would feel like, in one of these more impoverished countries, reading about what life could be like, in some other country, under a less oppressive regime? Now imagine that not only can that person READ anything from elsewhere, they can also WRITE their personal experiences to the

Internet and the web, so that anyone, anywhere else can see what is going on in their lives.

We are seeing a small taste of these things today: look at all the tweets and YouTube videos which emanated from the violence surrounding the elections in Iran, and subsequent protests and riots. Without the Internet, and the ability for humans to WRITE to the web, as well and READ from it, we would have no idea what is going on over there. Think of when every human on the planet has a full read/write device.

This is deathly frightening to the state, as it subsists and survives (and this is important) on the restriction of the flow of information from one person to another. If there truly were a free flow of information from anyone to anyone, why would we need a state?

Why are states even necessary? As far as I'm concerned, the state simply exists to retard the forward progress of humanity, not accelerate it. And once we get full two-way connectivity to most of the humans on the planet, then states will no longer be necessary.

Let humanity talk to each other, without restriction, and the world will change.

People Vs Party

The party is not the people, and hasn't been for a long time.

Witness the widespread discontent evidenced by the tea party movements which started in 2009, then add in the discontent amongst progressives turning against Obama and the Democrats, and you have a full blown, anti-party movement going on. More and more people every day are leaving their prospective parties and marking down their party affiliation as "Independent"

The problem, if you ask me, is that most people out there are unhappy with the progress of either of the parties out there for these reasons:

1. They are not really aligned with your interests
2. They say that they are aligned with your interests in order to get into power, then opportunistically change their tune once in power in order to solidify their power
3. They really are the both for the same goals, and neither is willing to listen to the people
4. While they fight on the surface and in the view of the cameras, they are really both only interested in the same thing: increasing their power, suppressing the people, and taking more of our money. They just do it for different reasons. Think of opposing lawyers who fight each other mercilessly in the courtroom, only to meet for drinks later after

their clients have gone home. This is Washington, and our State and Local governments today.

Even George Washington said:

"However [political parties] may now and then answer popular ends, they are likely in the course of time and things, to become potent engines, by which cunning, ambitious, and unprincipled men will be enabled to subvert the power of the people and to usurp for themselves the reins of government, destroying afterwards the very engines which have lifted them to unjust dominion."

Sounds like the parties of today, don't they? So what do people say: "Throw them all out! Both parties suck, so we need a third party to come in there and clean house". Problem is is that will never happen: the current duopoly has things so locked down that a third (or fourth or fifth) party could not possibly win enough of anything to get into power. I saw this in action during Bill Clintons election. Remember Ross Perot? Sure, millions voted for him, but he didn't even get ONE vote in the electoral college. Same thing will happen to any other future movement.

This is why, even though I hate to say it, the only way we can effect real change, real movement back to the founding principles of this country, is to infect members from BOTH parties with the ideals WE hold dear. We need to identify leaders in both parties who feel like we do, and get them voted in, no matter if they are Democrat, Republican, or Independent. A "block" not a party. A block who believes as we do.

People Vs Media

When was the last time you turned on the TV, turned on the radio, or picked up the newspaper, and liked what you saw?

Ever since the "Savior" – Barack Hussein Obama, came onto the scene, way back at the Democratic convention of 2004, the media and the progressive movement has been in absolute, abject love with this guy. He has gotten way more exposure and positive press than any other political candidate in the history of American politics. Considering the way he was and IS being treated by the press, I'd almost say that the adulation goes beyond politics. I mean, is this guy really more popular than Michael Jackson, The Beatles and Jesus combined?

I wonder if the media noticed the correlation between the over the top love for this man (who if you ask me – and most people out there, is simply a YAP – "Yet Another Politician") and the decline in circulation of viewers for their newspaper or the viewers of their programs?

The journalists did not do their industry any favors, catering to and presenting their new progressive hero in a glowing light, at all times, even when he said things that we worth investigating. Look at all the supporters, like the Reverend Wright, who he "threw under the bus" when it looked like he was not really helping his campaign. Where was the investigation there?

Sure, you say, the Internet has contributed to the death of traditional media in many ways. This is true.

I'd much prefer to view programming online, read my news there, and maybe catch a movie on streaming Netflix, or a TV show on Hulu, or by and download a program that I missed on Apple TV.

But the unending torrent of adulation for this YAP, which continues to this day (the day I am writing this – and probably to the day you are reading this) won't help to return journalism to its former glory. If you ask me, that whole industry is dead, replaced by citizen bloggers.

Of course, now that Obama's stock is at its lowest ebb, he is about an unpopular as Bush, the mainstream media continues to support him, to the detriment of their audiences.

The mainstream media is pretty much beyond irrelevant now.

It would probably be a good idea to just stop listening/reading/watching it, period.

Audio Vs Video

I've done both a podcast (and radio show, if you can call a library of over 900 episodes a radio show), and at TV show (if you can call a YouTube channel with over 300 videos a TV show) and I feel that I have to say something about the different audiences.

I just find that people who listen to my radio show much much much smarter than people who watch my show.

Now, I don't mean to belittle people who prefer either medium. I'm sure that there are plenty of really smart, erudite viewers of my TV show, and plenty of dull, dim-witted listeners of my radio show. None of the dumb ones are reading this book so I don't really need to be nice to you here, but if you are, then you know who you are.

My listeners and viewers are on the most part, pretty smart. They get that I don't shill for one party or the other, that I push for everyone to be smart enough to not just follow along with the crowd, to use your brain, to research things for yourself, and all that good stuff.

I just don't get why most of the comments I get on my radio show are smart, reasoned arguments, and most of the comments I get on my TV show are profanity laden taunts about never getting laid, living in my parents basement, kissing George Bush's ass, being unemployed, and/or all of the above.

Maybe it has something to do with YouTube, or maybe it the demographics of YouTube, or maybe it's the paid Obama operatives going around defending their man.

Personally, I think that people who listen to the radio are actually engaged in more than one thing at a time, and have better imaginations, whereas people who watch TV have to sit in front of it and do nothing but watch. So the radio listeners have bigger better brains, more synapses firing, more ideas, more innovative etc.

And the YouTube watchers are probably watching me from their parent's basements, wondering if anyone will love them, or if they will ever get Obama to pay for their gas and mortgage.

Just a thought. I could be wrong.

Talk Vs Action Culture

I'm a native of Canada – if you listen or watch my shows you'll know that. I moved to the US in 1998, and became a citizen of the US in November of 2007.

One of the things we LOVE to do in Canada is complain about things. It's often known as the national pastime, either before hockey or tied with hockey. Don't even get me started with bitching about hockey! So whenever we see anything which is, let's say, less than optimal, the first thing Canadians do is complain. However, they don't complain out in the open. That wouldn't be very Canadian. They usually just grumble to themselves.

Example: when a driver cuts you off, instead of opening your window and shouting at them, you grumble about the other driver, to yourself, or in a low tone that no one else can hear. Or if someone buts in line ahead of you, you just sit there and grumble to yourself quietly, and let them take the spot ahead of you. Canadians are bred to be so polite and docile, that you can do almost anything to a Canadian, and he/she will just take it. This is, in my opinion, pretty standard socialist country stuff: they don't really want the populace to be anything more than docile. The government breeds that kind of behavior into you, through years and years of schooling and media bombardment. Americans are rude and coarse, they say, and Canadians are nice and polite. Thus preparing the way for a docile populace which will take any direction.

America, on the other hand, is pretty much the opposite. Let me demonstrate:

When I first moved here, I was struck by a very simple incident. The company I was working for at the time took us all out for a concert at an outdoor theater here in Silicon Valley. While we were waiting in line to get into the theater, my boss and I were discussing the news of the day. At that moment, someone stepped into line ahead of my boss. Like I mentioned, in Canada, we'd grumble a bit and go back to what we were saying. So witnessing this, I was prepared to grumble with my boss about this and go back to my conversation. To my surprise (I know, as Americans this is not a surprise), he turned to the interloper and said sternly "Hey, Buddy, the back of the line is back there" and pointed. The guy looked at him and said "Sorry" then went to the back of the line.

Now you are probably thinking, so what. I do that every day. But guess what: it's a cultural thing. Americans are bred to TAKE ACTION. When they see an injustice take place, they don't simply grumble about it, as Canadians and many other socialist cultures do, they step up and take action to correct the injustice. You see it everywhere. All the time. It's so inbred into American culture that you take it for granted:

1. When you see a stranded car you stop to help
2. When a tsunami hits Indonesia, or an earthquake hits Haiti, you open your wallets.
3. Hell, some of you even drop everything and head down there to personally help

4. When a purse is stolen, you chase down the thief and get it back

This is what we would do in Canada:

1. When you see a stranded car we drive right by and think – someone else can help
2. When a tsunami hits Indonesia, or an earthquake hits Haiti, we look to the UN to throw some cash their way
3. We hope that the government drops a few things and sends people down there to help
4. When a purse is stolen, we look the other way and hope the victim didn't see us do that.

America has an action culture. Canada, and many, many other socialist states, have a talk culture. Those cultures weren't always like that: their overarching socialist governments over time have turned their citizens into that.

Unfortunately this is the way America is heading. Starting with Roosevelt (some would argue even further back), and including most of the administrations since then, government scope and size have been expanding, and our freedoms and income after taxes have been decreasing.

And the only challenge to the injustices which government foists upon us is met by the resolve and actions of the American people, who have still been bred to act.

Don't let them take that away from us.

Survivor Vs Apprentice

You know, I used to watch both Survivor and The Apprentice at one point in my life. I can reveal now that it was a pretty low point, but I did learn something from that experience.

First of all, if you have never watched either of these programs, here is a recap:

Survivor: (ain't Wikipedia great?)

Survivor is a reality television game show format produced in many countries throughout the world. In the show, contestants are isolated in the wilderness and compete for cash and other prizes. The show uses a system of progressive elimination, allowing the contestants to vote off other tribe members until only one final contestant remains and wins the title of "sole survivor". The format for survivor was created in 1992 by Charlie Parsons. The show is credited for making reality television a popular TV genre.

The Apprentice: (again, Wikipedia)

The apprentice is a television franchise which originated in 2004 in the United States. As originally conceived, the show depicted 16 contestants from around the country with various backgrounds competing in an elimination-style competition to become an apprentice to Donald Trump. The winning contestant would have the opportunity to work for trump as the president of one of his companies for at least one year with an annual salary of $250,000.

Now some of you are thinking, so what? Reality TV sucks, but we are all into it, right. Like American Idol, everyone loves to see people win and lose right? Everyone loves to see competitions where we can cheer one side or the other. It's why we watch sports as well.

But there is a big, big difference between these two programs. One rewards the worst in us, and the other one rewards the best.

In Survivor, the winner is selected and rewarded by being the nastiest. The player who can manipulate the other players the best is usually the one who wins the prize.

In The Apprentice, like in real business, well, the way business is supposed to be, the one who does the best job wins. It's a meritocracy, where Survivor is a "nastiocracy"

Unfortunately, our culture is starting to love rewarding the nasty, manipulative back-stabbing better than rewarding the industrious hard worker. It's a sad day in America where we cheer the backstabber over the businessman, the person who was able to cheat their way to the top over the person who was able to claw their way to the top through hard work. We cheer the manipulator, and curse the hard worker.

I'm sure that's not what the founders were thinking when they set this all up, 200 or so years ago, did they?

Celebrities Are Aliens

Ahh, celebrities. Where would we be without them? Better off I'm sure.

You see, celebrities really are aliens. Maybe at some point they were human, probably before they were celebrities.

I'm not sure what's worse, the fact that people look up to these people, or the lives of these people.

Do you guys remember Men in Black? It was a great movie with Will Smith and Tommy Lee Jones. At one point during that film, they intimated that all celebrities are aliens. I tend to agree.

Maybe the reason they all act so crazy is that they understand that their reign is slowly coming to an end. Like all incredible shifts in the world, the internet is creating celebrities out of real people. And these real people are staying more real than ever before. So yes, maybe the time for crazy celebrities is over.

Have you ever seen a real celebrity in real life? First of all, they are all like tiny versions of real people. None of them are normal size. Maybe it has something to do with fitting on the screen or something. Even those celebrities who look huge are really little people.

Have you ever listened to a celebrity talk about politics, or global warming, or health care, or the environment, or any issue other than what they really know how to do, like sing or act? I mean really, why does anyone listen to a celebrity on any topic other than those? What gives them the ability to opine on these topics with any more gravitas than your neighbor Phil? In fact, I'd say that Phil may know even more than Tom Cruise of the topic of health care.

For example, what the heck does Oprah know about anything? Why do millions upon millions of people follow her every move, watch her every show, and buy every book she ever recommends? Is it because people think she is like them, that she can feel the same way they do? Get over yourself, people. Oprah, Obama, Tom Cruise, Madonna, and all of them. They are not like us. They can't get anywhere near what our life is like, just like we can't get anywhere near what their life is like.

It's like a Catholic priest giving marital advice. How does he know?

Stop walking in lockstep with the millions who are following your favorite celebrity along with you. Are you really like them, or are they really like you? Think about it. They can't help you live your life.

Only you can live your life.

The State Makes Your Wildest Dreams Come True

There was a scene in Napoleon Dynamite, where Pedro, who had to stand up in front of the whole school and make a speech, had trouble figuring out what to say. So he was told to say "elect me, and all your wildest dreams will come true". So when the time came, that what he said.

It's what politicians have done from the dawn of time. Vote for me and I will set you free, and many variations of the above have been told to prospective voters from the time of the first elections, way back in ancient Greece, or even earlier, I don't remember my history all that well.

The fact is, no one is responsible for making our wildest dreams come true except for ourselves. You know, that was part of the whole idea of America. That no one else is responsible for you but you.

This is way the founders basically said: Listen, we don't know what the future holds, we don't know what's best for you, we don't know what kind of life you want to lead, or want to want to do with your life, or what makes you happy, so I'll tell you what, we are going to set things up so that everyone is free to can do their own thing, follow their own path to happiness, as long as it doesn't hurt others. We aren't giving you anything. We are giving you the opportunity "do it yourself".

If you want to spend your life amassing riches, go ahead. If you want to spend your life helping the poor, be my guest. America is the proverbial Big Tent, with room for everyone.

America is the ultimate DIY project. Everyone gets the opportunity to make their wildest dreams come true.

Unfortunately, many of us have forgotten that. Especially since many politicians over the last hundred years have told us repeatedly "we can do it for you, just relax". This is, of course, a lie, and completely anathema to what the founders intended.

Whether it's running schools into last place in the world, to banning organic farming, the state has repeatedly proven that they do not follow the people's wishes.

Only you can make your wildest dreams come true, and pretty much the only place you still have the opportunity to do it is still right here.

Government FAIL

When was the last time the state succeeded at anything? I mean seriously, can anyone really point at anything, even ONE thing, that the state is doing and say, wow, you guys really know what you are doing? I mean, I can't even think of one example which is better off in the hands of the state. Can you?

- DMV
- Medicare
- War on Drugs
- War on Poverty
- Abu Ghirab
- No Child Left Behind
- Katrina And FEMA
- Socialized Medicine
- Cap & Trade
- The Stimulus Bill...

Man, I could go on and on and on. There is not ONE thing I can think of which is better off in the hands of the state, except for those few things that the founders outlined specifically in the Constitution. Remember the Tenth Amendment:

The powers not delegated to the United States by the Constitution, nor prohibited by it to the States, are reserved to the States respectively, or to the people.

There you have it. Unless it specifically states it in the Constitution, the federal government has absolutely no say in any or all of the above. In fact, despite the thousands and thousands of pages of Federal Laws (who knows how many there are! I tried to find out by searching the internet and the best answer I could get was that there were 134,723 pages of regulations in the Federal Register back in 1998! That was more than 10 years ago – and BEFORE 9/11. Can you imagine what the number of laws is like now? We don't even know how many laws there are PER page! No one knows the answer.) The reality is that the only true laws that the federal government is supposed to have jurisdiction over are outlined right there in the Constitution. The rest are to be from the states or the people. Of course, the states have gone nuts with new laws and regulations as well.

I don't know about you, but having a literally uncountable number of laws on the books is not just a punch to the gut of liberty, but a full frontal assault.

And of those hundreds of thousands of laws and regulations, which actually work. I'd venture to say that the number of laws that were in place in 1925 (one slim volume) were probably good enough.

We live in a police state right now, and that should bother you, no matter if you are a Democrat or a Republican, Progressive or Conservative. When the state takes away our rights and freedoms, everyone suffers.

Gaping Maw of the State

So, not only does the state fail at everything that they attempt to accomplish, they also spend ridiculous amounts of our money doing it. If you think about each and every government program that has gone into effect in the last 100 years, they all have two things in common

1. They are completely or mostly ineffective
2. They are stupidly expensive

The examples are legion, but I'll throw you a recent one just for laughs. The Stimulus Bill, which cost approximately 800 billion dollars of our tax money, was supposed to reduce the unemployment rate by a specific amount, or at least insure that the unemployment rate would not go above a certain level.

In the promises, Obama said that it would "create or save 4 million jobs" Now, considering you can't really track job "saving", I guess that was his way out of bailing on it if it didn't work. And like I said, the state is in a perpetual state of failure, and an expensive failure at that. When it did actually create jobs, the tiny number of jobs that it did create "25 cops here, 100 fire-fighters there, 500 construction workers etc" would mean that the cost to create each job would be in the multi-millions. Hell, at 800 billion, you could have given each and every unemployed person assuming that there were really 4 million jobs lost, $200,000 EACH. Now that would be doing something (instead of just paying off his cronies for helping him get elected, which is the REAL reason for the stimulus bill), imagine 4 million NEW businesses, 4 million new entrepreneurs, each with a tidy $200k in startup funds. The recession would be over with a snap of the fingers.

At last count, the net job loss since the "stimulus bill" went into law is 25 million. That is 25 million jobs lost since Obama came into power. And many of those jobs are never coming back, at least until government is pared back.

But the state does not want the people to help themselves. Doing so would put them out of a job.

Take things like building a building, or any project for that matter. If you look at how governments build compared to how private enterprises build, the differences are amazing. The businesses need to build things as efficiently as possible so that they can minimize the time and cost of putting the building up, thereby saving their shareholders money, and keeping enough in the bank to keep going through the lean times, etc. When a government builds a building or does some kind of works project, the cost overruns are literally insane. I came across this table the other day (Reason March 2010):

Project	Est. $	Act. $	Overrun %
Boston's "Big Dig"	$2.6B	$98B	3669%
Medicare	$12B	$98B	716%
Kennedy Center Parking Lot	$28M	$88M	214%
Capitol Hill Visitor Center	$265M	$621M	134%

Can you see any private enterprise surviving with cost overruns in the hundreds or thousands of percent? The "Big Dig" went over schedule by 7 years! Can you really see any project managers or their groups at private companies getting away with anything even near that? Haven't you ever noticed that when a private enterprise builds anything, whether it's a commercial space or housing, it goes up in record time? But when the government does it, it takes forever? I mean, come on, it even takes the government twice as much time and money to build a frigging parking lot! Even the ode to themselves cost more than double the original cost. Can you imagine Joe Taxpayer, working hard, half his salary ripped out of his wallet by the myriads levels of government, happily visiting a center in a dank basement celebrating government excess?

And you wonder why there is a tea party movement.

Socialized Health Care or ObamaCare

This is a really important issue, so I'm not joking around on this one. Take it from me, I have experienced socialized health care for the first 35 years of my life, and I have to tell you, it is the worst thing that could happen to America. Here are some of the reasons why.

1. If the state can barely run anything properly, why would we expect that the state can run anything like our bodies properly? Because that is what we would be doing, ceding control of our bodies and our lives to the state.
2. Did you know that a lot of the propaganda about how wonderful socialized medicine is a lie. People like Michael Moore purposely mess around with facts in order to further their cause.
3. Did you know that this will change our quality of care for the worse?
4. Did you know that the cost of health care will skyrocket, you just won't know by how much anymore, since the massive costs will be hidden in your taxes.
5. Death panels will be a reality. This is absolutely 100% true, they just don't call them that.
6. Procedures will not be decided upon by your medical professionals, but by a committee of

bureaucrats. What do they know about the right treatment?

7. The state will have a real interest in reducing health care costs. This will lead to things like them taking a very active interest in our lifestyles and our bodies. Here come the mandatory, early morning jumping jacks as we sing paeans to our savior.

8. The heavy new tax burden will crush our optimistic culture

That last point is the most important. You see, most people don't see the big picture. They have a paper thin understanding of what ObamaCare is all about. They watch and read about how "wonderful" the "free" health care systems are in other countries, and the media and propagandists like Michael Moore take examples of poor health care here, and examples of great health care there and just present those. The fact of the matter is that America still has the best health care system in the world.

People from all over the world, rich, poor and middle class, come to America to get the best of care. Where do you think Arab sheiks go when they need a procedure? Or Canadian who can't get health care in their home province go? People travel to the US to get care. If the health care sucked here – then why would people travel here to get it?

If the care in Canada and Cuba is so great – why don't you hear stories of conjoined twins, and famous international celebrities, go to Cuba for care? The fact is that they come to the US for a reason – we have the best health care system bar none – and one of the reasons we have the best system is that it still pays some attention to the free market.

In every other country, where the health care is poor – it is socialized to some degree or another. Injecting bureaucratic government processes into something which craves innovation to survive – like health care – will kill all innovation in health care.

Case in point – look at the time and money it takes for a new drug to get to market. This is an area where the government has dug deep into an industry. Time and cost keep all sorts of interesting drugs off the market. I bet there are a number of interesting cures out there which are being kept away from us due to the FDA.

But I digress: Beyond the fact that any socialized health care system will most likely cost a lot of money, and provide worse care (when have you ever heard that the states intervention in an industry making it better?), the extra burden that it will carry on our society will completely crush our spirit. Has there been any other legislation which basically gives the state control over our bodies? That the simple act of being alive in the US will require compliance? That if you do not comply with the payment of premiums, you can be thrown in jail. Jail time for simply living in the United States, and choosing to not contribute to the health costs of others.

The immense costs of this type of system cannot be understated. Each and every country where socialized medicine exists, the costs are so out of control – since there is no free market to rein them in – that it is standard practice to deny treatments to people for cost reasons. Isn't that the exact same things that Obama wants to stop? So instead of insurance companies denying PAYMENT for a procedure, the power will be in the hands of the state to deny the procedure – period – no recourse. In the current system, you can still scrounge up enough money to pay for it – even if the insurance company denies payment. Under ObamaCare – if they deny you – you will have to leave the country if you want to get the treatment at all. This is exactly want many Canadians do. In fact, recently the Premier (like a state Governor) of Newfoundland went to the US to get a heart procedure done because the procedure was simply not available to him in Canada. And trust me, this guy wasn't poor.

The costs cause the system to either deny treatments, or, because the waiting list is so immense, delay them so far as to make them pointless. For example, in some places in Canada, it takes 10 months to get a pre-natal screening. People have literally died in Canada, waiting for a "free" life saving treatment, when they could have crossed the border and gotten treatment before they died, but for a price.

Even Canadian Premiers (basically the same as state governors) have to travel to the US in order to get treatment. Some treatments are basically completely unavailable in Canada. Is this what you want here as well - governments dictating which treatments you can/cannot have at any price?

And finally, I want to recount a little conversation with a true Obama-ite on ObamaCare. Here was our dialog:

Me: Did you know that under socialized medicine, you may have to wait on a waiting list for treatment for a life saving procedure, where you could just travel to the states and get it done right away for a price?

Him: I'd much rather die than leave my family in debt

Me: Are you serious?

Him: Yes

Me: So you are saying that if your wife or child were sick and needed treatment right away, otherwise they would die, you'd rather wait and get the treatment for free, than try to borrow the money somehow now and get the treatment so that they could live?? (I asked incredulously)

Him: Yes (Dead serious)

When you have complete fanatics like this (see my nugget on Fanatics) running things like health care, you can understand why things which we thought were anathema to the American people, like death panels, are perfectly reasonable.

My friends, the debate has been hijacked by the crazy, and we need to take it back.

Taxes, "Sin" and Otherwise

Back in Canada, the land of high taxes in which I spent the first 35 years of my life, we had these lovely things called "sin taxes". Sin taxes, as they were dubbed – actually I'm not sure who by, since it could have been some witty Canadian writer, reporter or journalist – were taxes on the following:

1. Booze (that's alcohol to you Americans)
2. Smokes (cigarettes – cigars don't count)
3. Gas (yes, that stuff you put in your car)

So booze. Yes, I guess that's the main reason that they called it a "sin" tax, in this fairly puritan white bread, Christian society, it was a sin to drink. So they figured, why not tax the crap out of it. I mean, we don't really want people to drink do we? Not only is it bad for you morally, it also causes all sorts of medical problems and diseases and accidents, all things which need to be paid for in the land of "free" socialized health care. This is why it costs; I kid you not, about $40-50 for a bottle of cheap vodka in the Great White North. A bottle you could get in the States for about $10.

Smokes. Sure, smoking is really bad for you – it's been proven right? (Well, at least smoking tobacco has) A small pack of cigarettes is over $10 I think right now. At one point, they had a terrible smuggling problem in Canada, a number of native tribes were into smuggling them across the border from the US, when you could buy a pack of cigarettes for $2 in the US and sell them for $10 in Canada, pretty good markup, eh? It was a terrible problem, people were getting killed, and it was awful. So the government at the time did something really crazy. It reduced the tax on the packs so that they were about $3. It completely killed the smuggling since it wasn't worth the smugglers while to bring those in. Of course, over time its back up again, since the government couldn't survive without the tax revenues

And finally gas. Since where is it a sin to drive your car? One could argue that Canada had a so-called carbon tax before anyone else. Yay Canada, eh? Guess how much gas has been in Canada for ages? $3 a gallon gas is cheap in Canada. Lately it's been nearly $5 a gallon, and of course whenever the government needs more cash, "sin taxes" are the first that go up, because we all know it's a sin to drive a car in this world.

Why am I telling you this? You're thinking, nah, that will never happen here. Right. Remember, the gaping maw of government? If this administration is hell-bent on going down the same socialist path that wrecked all of these other nations, you can bet all of this stuff is in our future.

Don't forget the most heinous of all. The GST, a federal sales tax on nearly everything, has been in place in the UK, Canada, and many of the other countries Obama seems to idolize. If he wants to bring all of these socialist "wonders" to Americans, eventually they WILL have to be paid for. All we have to do is look north to figure out WHO will pay.

Criminal Aliens

I tell you, as someone who went through the pain and suffering to become a LEGAL citizen of the United States, nothing burns my ass more than rewarding those people who come into this country illegally.

There are thousands of us who honor the laws of the country we wish to live in. We fill out forms, pay our money, wait patiently in line, get jobs, pay taxes, and hope and pray that the bureaucrat adjudicating our case is having a good day. Cause if they are not, we could be summarily banned for 5 years.

Millions of others simply cross the border, either under cover or come in and allow their status to expire. They are then given free everything, since they usually work in cash only businesses, do not have to pay taxes, and then every ten years or so, some idiot president, sensing that this is the next big demographic that will vote for him since he gives them amnesty, proposes amnesty.

Can you imagine the rage and pain we feel when we see things like this? There are literally hundreds of thousands of hard-working, law-abiding people who are trying to emigrate, and have emigrated, to this country legally. Those people are treated like criminals, suspiciously, simply because not only do we want a better life for ourselves and our families, we want to work to support America, since we deeply understand what sets it apart from the rest of the world, what makes it special.

Can you imagine the pain, when a hard working engineer has to wait years in order to re-unite with his family, when the lawbreaking illegal alien is not only GIVEN citizenship, they are allowed to immediately bring their families into the country.

The current immigration system punishes the law follower and rewards the law breaker. This is why I call those who are in this country what they really are "criminal aliens", since "undocumented immigrants" does not really expose the truth about them.

Why should the immigration laws hold any less power than any other law? Why do we feel sorry for these law breakers as opposed to every other type?

So that's why I say, call them what they are: **CRIMINALS**.

But I have a solution.

Too bad no one has the guts to implement it.

Proof Positive That America Is the Best Place on Earth

America is the best place on earth.

Yup, I said it.

And now I'm going to prove it. How? Very simple:

America is what people want.

What you say? How do you know it's what people want? Simple. We reduce it all down to math and facts. And you all know, unlike opinion, math and facts don't lie. Well, at least they have never lied to me.

The UN every now and then undertakes world migration studies. Basically, what they do is track the movement of people within countries, and migration of people from country to country. It's all statistics, they never asked people why they did something, and they just looked at the numbers of people who moved from one place to the other. Sounds pretty simple right?

Here is what they found:

1. People always move from less free countries to more free countries. You don't see a lot of migration from places like France to Saudi Arabia. Or from the US to China.
2. People move to the United States more than any other country, by a very wide margin. In fact, I think that the US is so far out ahead of all these other countries and even if you

combined all the rest, the US would still be near the top.

So what does this tell us?

1. People, in general, want to be free
2. People want to live an American life.

Yup, irrefutable proof is right there. How can you argue with it? Its pure math and fact. There are no opinions even asked.

I mean, the only way that you can really question this is to say that the UN could be wrong, and that they are purposely fudging the numbers in order to make America look better. Seriously? When have you ever seen the UN do ANYTHING to make America look better? So it's a fact of life: People all over the world, most human beings wherever they live, want to live an American life.

Think about it for a second. If most people want to live an American life, and most people want freedom, shouldn't that be the ideal we all strive for? Why are these progressive politicians, no matter which party they are from, trying to bring these things, like socialized medicine, high taxes, social programs and the like, to America, when the rest of the world is fleeing them? I fled them. Most immigrants, whether legal or illegal, are here fleeing the very thing Obama and his ilk are trying to bring here.

I say, give an American life to them. If by a huge margin, most people want to live an American life, we should encourage other countries to be more American, not turn America into these other countries.

So we should be actively promoting freedom, capitalism and democracy around the world. We should be spreading America to the rest of the world, not remaking America in the image of the rest of the world.

But there's an important caveat: you can't take these ideals and shove them down people's throats at the point of a gun, like Bush did with Iraq. If these countries want to be free, if they really want to be more America-like (not American) then we should help the people in those countries free themselves. Give them the resources to liberate themselves, don't liberate them. If we do that: they own the freedom. It wasn't given to them. And they will realize how precious that freedom is. Well, they probably already know that, assuming that any reports of what it's like in America get back to the people.

America: Not On Prozac

Many people opine that America is a harsh place. That if you don't have a job, that if you don't have a home or skill, or if you are disadvantaged in any way, that it's very difficult to survive and to flourish. It's easy to get by if you have a job, your health insurance is paid for, and you can live your life in relative peace. But, if something goes wrong, there is no "safety net" to catch you. When you fail in America, you fail spectacularly.

On the flip side, however, you can also succeed incredibly. The same lack of safety net at the bottom of the ladder also means that there is no limit to what you can achieve. So in the other direction, there is nothing holding you back. You can be a spectacular success, or a spectacular failure.

And unless the Obama administration changes something radically, that is one of the awesome things about America.

I liken it to Prozac. If you know anything about Prozac, or any of those anti-depressants for that matter, they work by softening the peaks and valleys of people's moods. Think of peoples moods like a sine wave: you can be really happy (peak of wave) or really sad (valley of wave), or somewhere in between. Being in between is kind of where your doctor wants you to be. So when they developed Prozac, what it did was chop off the really low moods, and the really high moods, effectively putting a ceiling on the happiness, but also putting a floor on the sadness, which is more important anyways.

So what does this have to do with politics? Simple. In other countries, it's like they took a giant Prozac: sure they catch you if you fail spectacularly, via the "safety net" programs, like welfare. But they also stop people from succeeding spectacularly, but purposely chopping down the most successful, by taxing them very heavily. Thus, these countries, while they may stop you from failing, they also stop you from succeeding.

This is a risk, for sure. One of the biggest reasons America is so successful, in every way, is that its people get the opportunity to be an amazing success. Sure, it comes at the risk of possibly being a colossal failure, but at least here you get that chance. Everywhere else, if you are a success, they tear you down. They penalize success.

And if we aren't careful, they will do the exact same thing to America.

Immigration

You know, it's really funny. For some reason, the whole idea of immigration or fixing the immigration process seems to freak people out. On the one hand, you have millions of Americans who are worried about losing their jobs to foreigners who come to the US, and on the other hand you have a need for educated workers. You also understand that our society benefits from the influx of immigrants: legal immigrants that is.

You've heard many pundits expound that America is "a nation of immigrants". So we are: most Americans, myself included, are from somewhere else.

So as an American "from somewhere else" let me make a really simple suggestion on how to solve the immigration "problem"

First, the problem is not with immigrants and immigration. LEGAL immigration leads to positive benefits across the board. Societies grow and evolve and improve as new members arrive from outside of the society and adopt that society as their own. As long as the American "Melting Pot" continues, and we don't slide into multiculturalism, the diversity disease which seems to be sweeping all these other socialist states and creating hellish social issues (remember all of those riots in France – multiculturalism is the cause)

No the problem is not immigration – the problem in ILLEGAL immigration. It's funny how the progressive journalists accuse the conservative journalists or being against immigration in general, when it's more likely that what they are really objecting to is in the illegal immigration (please see nugget CRIMINAL ALIENS)

But I'm digressing again: the problem really is simple.

1. The process to legally enter the country is HORRIBLE. I went through so many hoops in order to become a legal immigrant to the United States, it's no wonder that many come here illegally. It took me 10 years, thousands of dollars, 5 different kinds of VISAs and permits in order to become a citizen. Trust me, it's tough.

2. There are way too many immigrants here illegally. People say that there isn't anything that can be done other than a pure amnesty – which angers me intensely. After spending all that time, money and suffering in order to become a citizen, the simple thought that these people were going to simple be handed on a silver platter what I busted my ass to accomplish for years just filled me with rage. Does America really stand to punishing those who follow the rules and reward those who don't? But there is a solution.

Here is the solution. It is so incredibly simple that no one has the cojones to implement it. Plus the whole illegal immigration industry would be thrown into turmoil. Where would the rich be if they would have to pay their legal American gardeners a fair salary, as opposed to under market prices for illegal immigrants:

1. Improve the immigration process. Instead of having people jump through 100 hoops to become a citizen, bring it down to one or two. Ideally, if someone wishes to become a US citizen, they should be able to apply and get approved or denied at the airport while they are waiting for their plane into the country. With the proper databases and information, immigration officials should be able to approve not just entry but citizenship immediately

2. DEPORT EVERYONE! Send everyone who is not a legal citizen of this country right back to where they came from. Immediately. Just round them up and ship them back. No fines (except maybe for cost to transport them back), no jail time. Just send them all back to their home countries.

That's it. If someone who is sent back wishes to come back to America, then all they need to do is to come back, and go through the new, improved immigration process as outlined in Step 1.

This WILL work. If we do this, everyone coming in to work and use the services of this country will be a legal immigrant – and even citizen of this country.

Color Blind Society

You know, when I grew up in Canada, I don't think I really saw anything like racism. But then again, I experienced something different. Something I think was called a "color-blind society."

To me that meant that it didn't matter what you looked like, you were judged on your words and deeds, not your appearance.

In fact, our high school in Canada was fairly multiracial. But no one treated anyone any differently based on how they looked. Well, except maybe if you were ugly. Or maybe didn't like the same music. These were the 80s, BTW.

Like any school, we had our "cliques". But they had nothing to do with "race". At our school it was all about the music you liked. The kids who listened to punk hung out with the kids who also listened to punk, the rockers with the rockers etc. The New Wave folks were the ones with the Flock Of Seagulls haircuts (that was me, actually). There were no racial lines, as far as I could tell.

In a color-blind society, which if you ask me, is the intended end result of a post-racial society, race does not matter. Everyone is treated exactly the same way, no matter what they are. It is a true end to racism.

However, we do not live in a color blind society. The only reason why we do not live in a color blind society, which, as I said, is the true end of racism, is that the "races" (personally, I don't believe in the word "race" – I believe that there is only one race –

that is the HUMAN race – and we are all a part of that) which felt oppressed before, now want revenge against the races which oppressed them. Equality is not enough. There must be payback, even though those who committed the crimes are long gone.

It's not enough that the "races" now CAN be on an equal footing. The "white race" must now be punished for the crimes of its ancestors

So instead of true equality among the "races", aka a color-blind society, we simply continue to be racist, only this time, someone else is being oppressed.

How does this make us more enlightened? How does this improve humanity?

It doesn't. The only way that we can step beyond racism, the only way to a post-racial society is not to elect a multi-racial candidate who identifies with African-Americans and encourages racist talk, but to treat everyone equally, to truly become a color-blind society.

Racism: Nature Wants Us Intermarried

You know, since the first multi-racial (yes, folks, why do I seem to be the only one who remembers that fact – everyone else seems to have forgotten that he had a white mother) candidate was installed in the White House, the word "racism" has been used a whole heck of a lot, usually by people who really have no other way of defending indefensible positions that Obama takes on many issues. Here is the usual exchange:

Citizen A: "I'm not happy with Obama's policy on health care"

Citizen B: "Racist!"

Can you guess which just wants to express an opinion and who wants to suppress an opinion? But I digress.

At the core, libertarianism is about people. Not white, black, yellow, green, but people.

We are talking about basic human rights, as encoded by the founders in the Constitution. There was no mention of white, black, yellow, green, male, and female, Jew or Gentile anywhere in the Constitution. It states simply:

We hold these truths to be self-evident, that all men are created equal, that they are endowed by their

Creator with certain unalienable Rights, that among these are Life, Liberty, and the Pursuit of Happiness.

There is no special mention of race, creed, religion. In fact, the amendments go on to specifically state that there is NO state religion, and that the people are free to worship as they see fit.

There is no racism in the Constitution. There is no sexism in the Constitution. There is no special dispensation if you are part of this or that group. It is all about people, taking responsibility for themselves. Nowhere does it say that we should discriminate between this or that, unlike the Bible.

But my point was that Nature wants us the races to be intermarried. You are probably thinking, okay Future, I've read this far, but now you have Stopped Making Sense (which BTW was an awesome Talking Heads song). Hear me out for a second.

Have you ever noticed the usually the product of a interracial marriage tends to be very good looking? Take for example someone like Halle Berry, who is half white/half black. Or Freddie Prinze Jr. Or Paula Abdul. Or Jordin Sparks. Or Mariah Carey. Or Naomi Campbell. Or even (ugh – believe it or not some people find him good-looking) Barack Hussein Obama. It's my contention that in the grand scheme of things, nature creates good looking babies from interracial couples in order to prod us to make more.

Is this a crazy thought? Think about it for a second. Nature makes the first born of a couple look a lot like the father when they are first born, so that the father can recognize the child as his own. Is it so far-fetched to consider that the reason interracial couples babies are better looking is that nature wants more of those? Even from a purely scientific racial survival angle, the human race can only survive and become hardier through the most cross racial "pollination" so to speak. Genetics evolve as the bad stuff dies out and the good stuff continues.

Eventually, the human race will all be a blend of all three major races. In realty, if you ask me, there really is no such thing as "racism" – since there really is only one race.

The human race.

The United Nations

Ah, the UN. For the longest time I wondered, why are we still hosting these losers? And now I know. There has to be some group that ends up being the genesis of our "one world government"

This has always been the purview of the UN. For the longest time, the UN's influence and usefulness have been declining, as free markets and free peoples were on the ascent. But now that authoritarian regimes – like our own – are prevalent on this planet, its not a very far stretch to assume that one day the UN will grow to house the new "world government"

Remember all those sci-fi programs that we used to watch which postulated a one-world government which pretty much ran everything. In these programs, governments usually only came together due to some kind of external threat (like for example from some alien attack). Then all of Earth gets together, forgets about their "petty" squabbles, and defeats the bad guys. And of course, once the bad guys are defeated, they remain vigilant against external threat, but the one-world government remains.

What hogwash I'm thinking now. If anything, we need less government, less state, not more. What would the UN do for us, other than layer yet another layer of government over top what we already have. We are already laboring under at least 3 layers of government (as are most "civilized" countries) local, state, federal. Then add on regional (like the EU or the NAU), then throw the UN on top of that. That's 5 levels of government, touching every aspect of our lives. The world – a totalitarian state.

I'm not sure what to make of this North American Union discussion. One side of me says – yes it makes sense that there are states out there who want to create these uber states which can lord it over all the others. But on the flip side it requires that the state can foster and maintain something as sophisticated as a conspiracy to actually do this. My gut tells me that if this state doesn't even have the capability to deliver the mail – how can they possibly have the ability to maintain the secrecy around something as big as this. The state is a lumbering, stupid idiot, but is as ruthless as the Borg.

But progressives needn't worry.

Obama's next stop is "president of the world" anyways.

Market = Merit

Here is something else the state does which really annoys me. It's the various licenses and permits that are required to "be" someone or start a business.

It is my firm belief that the only indicator of someone's competence is the ability to do a thing, and to do that thing for money. For example, if you are capable of rerouting the plumbing pipes in a house, then you are a plumber. If you are capable of rewiring a house, then you are an electrician. If you are capable of building a wall, or a piece of furniture, then you are a carpenter. If you are capable of cooking a meal, then you are a caterer. Why do you need a piece of paper to prove that fact?

I mean, just think about how ridiculous it's become. Simply having the ability to DO a thing is not enough. Some agent of the state, some bureaucrat, needs to say "Yes you are an X", usually after you have papered their hands with cash.

For example, a few years ago I looked into the possibility of buying a piece of land a building a home on that. A custom home, built to my specifications, the way I wanted it.

Now I know a few things about building. I can build walls, route wires, run pipes, solder, glue etc. It's really not rocket science. I even dabbled in architecture at school. If life were fair, and we didn't have a ton of government intervention in our lives, I be able to buy this land, write up some plans and start building. I might need to hire some people to pour concrete and some other things I don't have the skills to do but for the most part I should be able to build my own house on my own terms.

Is this a free country? I'd need: zoning, permits, all contractors to have valid licenses, plans registered with the state on and on and on, adding tens or hundreds of thousands to the cost and months to the time involved. It turned out not to be worth the aggravation.

Some of you may say : "Well, it's the state which vets these people, makes sure that they know their skills, so that they don't do a poor job". I say BS. First of all, the state rarely ever tests these practitioners to see if they actually know their stuff, and secondly these permits and licenses are more a tax than permission or a skill assessment than anything else.

It's my contention, through these and other means, that it is the state, more than anything, that retards economic progress on every level. The other day, as I was picking up my kids from school, I envisioned a mini-bus service which picks up kids at school and drops them at home. Even a cursory look at all the rules and regulations and unions involved in such a venture made me think: damn: no wonder India and China are eating our lunch when it comes to commerce and innovation. We are just beset by so many oppressive rules and regulations we can't possibly compete.

We NEED freedom to operate. To invent. To work. To come up with and make money off new business ideas. And the state penalizes us at almost every turn on this.

There are only two ways around this. We can:

1. Expect the state to rescind all or most of these rules
2. Ignore them and go about our business

My guess is that the latter is the way to go – since I don't see the former ever happening.

The State Wants You Helpless

If you aren't helpless, then why should they exist?

If you think about it, why does the state exist at all?

If you go back to the reason that this country was founded – it was an escape from both economic and religious prosecution. The whole reason America was founded was to allow its citizens to enjoy a right to "life, liberty and the pursuit of happiness" in their own way. In a way it was a complete revolt against the state, in any form, and the true ascension of humanity, of the people. While originally the founders were very religious, they understood that it was the freedom to allow people to live their lives responsibly which was the special sauce that made America great.

However, as most good things do, they don't last, as there are always people who attempt to circumvent or wreck systems which they feel are unfair to others. While we did have an incredibly long period where there were minor attacks against the system and it was mostly weathered, we have seen the greatest expansion in government's size and scope in the last century. Why you ask?

Well it goes back to the UK, actually. The way I see it, all of this is rooted in the Poor Laws which came out of the UK. Apparently, during the Industrial Revolution, there was a huge upheaval in the world, since we were in the throes of transferring from an agrarian society to an industrial society. In this transition, there were many who left their villages to go work in factories and urban centers. In the process, some got jobs and were successful, and others weren't. Just like in nature, the strong do well and the weak perish, or at least wander the streets of London looking poor and disheveled. So one day, in coal smoke tinged London, two very proper gentlemen, most likely wealthy for generations, were walking from their homes to their gentleman's club one day in the fog. As they walked they came across some beggars in the streets, looked very dirty, and smelled bad. As they gazed upon them, one could imagine this conversation:

Gentlemen A: Oh my word, what do we have here?

Gentleman B: Seems to be a beggar. There are a lot of them about recently, haven't you noticed?

Gentleman A: Yes, actually I have, come to mention it. Well, what's London coming to? Used to be so civilized, and now there are all these beggars smelling up the joint. They don't look very appealing either, don't you agree?

Gentleman B: Agreed! But what can we do? Obviously the debtor's prisons are full, otherwise these unfortunates would be in them.

Gentleman A: Ack, well, if you ask me, I'd gladly give up a few schillings to get these degenerates off the streets! Not only would it improve the view, my old olfactories would surely thank me!

Gentleman B: Not a bad idea, old man! I shall bring it up at the next parliamentary session!

Gentleman A: Please do! As soon as you can, my friend.

And that's how it began. A couple of rich guys, probably rich from generations of theft, started the welfare system. The Poor Laws were passed in the UK, and the rich were taxed to feed the poor. This is one reason why their system is in much worse shape than ours, BTW, they started a heck of a lot earlier.

Oh yeah, I'm sure that Marx in is there somewhere as well. Anyways, long story short, eventually we ran into trouble here in the US around the start of the last century. Things were bad, but left on their own, and allowing the people to turn things around, would have probably shortened the Great Depression (a fact that many economists agree with today). But some enterprising president at the time (can you guess who?) basically used the crisis to turn the modern day Federal government and the Presidency into a pseudo-kingdom. And most successive Presidents, to this day, some more (Bush, Obama) than others (Reagan) have expanded the state in some way or another. The state originally existed for only two reasons:

1. Protect the rights of the American people
2. If there was an external threat to the country, organize resources, like armies, etc, in order to fend off invasion

That's it. The state was created assuming that people were individuals which could live their own lives, responsible adults who would, given the opportunity would be able to achieve great things. Of course, now the opposite is true: the state, instead of understanding that it is there to support the American people, and is there at the service of the American people, and that the American people can dissolve government at will, it has become its own behemoth which has a life of its own. Like Dr. Frankenstein losing control of his monster, we have lost control of this monster. And in the flip, it requires us to be helpless. If we are not helpless, if we have the ability to be responsible adults, it has no purpose. Part of governments will to live requires that we remain helpless. Once we are no longer helpless, we no longer need it.

And that is it's our biggest threat to it.

Safety Uber Innovation

Heck, flying cars would be here by now if it weren't for the state intervention in innovation

I used to record my show on my way to the office. You can probably watch me doing that. Back before the 2008 Presidential election, I used to record both my video show and my podcast on my way to the office, first by strapping my web cam onto my rear view mirror and doing my show while driving (got a lot of YouTube comments on that – believe me), and then once that show was done – usually 2-3 minutes, I'd switch over to my audio show and at my leisure, while I was driving, record my audio podcast the rest of the way, which ended up being between 30-40 minutes. Since I first started recording my show when I was on the road, my show sometimes had that flavor. Sometimes I would just break into a stream of profanities as someone cut me off, or some idiot in a big car who had no idea where they were going – I found that most people in SUVs think that they are so safe in them that they don't really care about what's going on around them.

But I digress. Being around cars all the time while I was recording my show taught me a few things:

1. Most people really do drive alone, to wherever they are going.
2. Most carpool lanes are usually empty, while the regular lanes are packed with slow moving traffic, probably belching out 6 times more carbon monoxide and wasting 10 times

more gas if they were just speeding by in the carpool lane. So carpool lanes are a big FAIL

3. Most cars are giant, lumbering metal cocoons which are way bigger than they need to be. I mean, really, do you really need a giant Hummer sized car in order to carry one 200 pound person 25 miles to work.

So, as an "inventor and futurist" (yes, folks, that's my day job title) I thought, cars could be made way better. So here is what I thought:

1. Why can't cars be modular? If you only need to carry one person, why can't they be the size of one person? If you want to travel with more than one person, connect in a second cabin, and sit with that person. Same for more than one. How many times do you take your 7 passenger Chrysler Behemoth out on your own in order to get a jug of milk? Just take your one module. Cars could conceivably expand and contract based on the need

2. Why do cars need to be SO armored? Made me think of football or hockey or any other professional sport. Back in the olden days, sure there were injuries, but it they weren't so bad, because it was mostly human piling on top of human, the padding, helmets etc where pretty light. Nowadays, these players take the field or ice with pounds and pounds of really tough equipment. This armor can do some damage. So suddenly everyone on the field or ice needs to wear the same level of protection.

Same goes for cars. Do we really need 750 layers or steel between ourselves and the outside world? The only reason cars are so damn armored is because some got armor, and now everyone wants an armored car to feel safe.

3. The Mommy state is here. We have all been infected with the Safety Virus. Since when do we all have to feel so God-damned safe and sound all the time? Driving a car IS dangerous. We should have to feel that danger.

And this is just one example. I can probably name hundreds of innovations that have been squashed in the name of safety by our nanny state. Take for example medicine: why does it take so many years for a drug to go from invention to actual humans? Because we are way too careful. Why can't we let people who could benefit from a drug make their own decision as to whether or not they wish to take the drug? Why do we have to let the state decide these things when it's not their life in the balance?

People are usually adults. We should treat them as such.

Video Games Teach Problem Solving Skills

One of the things I personally believe in incredibly important, a skill that everyone should have and cultivate, above all others, is the skill to problem solve.

Sure, public speaking is important. So is Language Arts, Math, Science etc. But if you ask me, once you have problem solving skills, then everything else falls out of that.

Here's an example: a number of years ago, I hired an intern to work on our IT dept at the company I was working at. The guys resume looked great, he had a certification in the type of network software we were using, and his credentials looked awesome. We interviewed him and he seemed to know his stuff. So we hired him and brought him in to work.

The very first task I gave him to do was to setup some computers, some of which had some issues. Judging by this guys educational credentials and experience, I figured that he would have all the work done in a few hours. A few hours later, I come back and find that he got completely stuck working on the first computer. So I sat with him and went over things with him. Left, then a few hours later came back. He had not moved on at all.

Eventually, as I watched him work, I realized that while he knew some things, and he followed instructions well, that the moment he ran into a snag, he got completely stuck. He had no way to get past the issue which he had come across. I realized that the thing this guy lacked was "problem solving skills" – the ability to figure out a solution to a problem that he came across. I realized that this was a skill that you can learn, and this guy, for all his credentials, didn't have that.

A year later, I hired another guy. No credentials whatsoever, but he had kick-ass problem solving skills. Even if he knew nothing about anything you set anything in front of him, he was able to figure it out, learn in the process, then solve more problems. That's when I realized, the core of everything, the core of all learning actually, is having problem solving skills. When you have good problem solving skills, nothing can faze you, since everything that comes at you is something you can figure out, whether it's driving, building a business, learning a new language, or making the country better.

In the past, kids learned problem solving skills in school or in real life: you were given problems in school, or in real life, and were expected to figure them out. Nowadays, the answers are fed to the students, and there are virtually no life lessons given.

I was a latecomer to video gaming: I had an old Nintendo Entertainment System in the garage, and only got back into it in 2002, with a Christmas purchase of a GameCube by my mom for my kids.

Video games had really moved on from the side scrolling shooting and sword play of Zelda. One of the games that came with the system was called Star Fox Adventures, an adventure style game, very visually beautiful, sort of in the vein of Legend of

Zelda, Ocarina of Time, a game I had skipped over since I dropped out of video gaming for a while.

However, I noticed something very interesting while I or my kids were playing this game: there were a ton of puzzles thrown into the mix along with the bashing and shooting. We worked together to solve each problem on the screen, moving blocks around etc. In the process I noticed that my kids were actually developing problem solving skills VIA playing the video game. And not only were they developing this skill, which I feel is the uber skill above all others, that they were having a great time doing it.

Contrast that to the dull instruction both adults and kids get learning nowadays.

Dude, where are our kids going to learn to solve problems, except for here?

Speaking Ill of the Dead

Something I don't understand, maybe someone can explain it to me. Seems that once people die, for some reason they always seem to be remembered much more fondly than they are in life. For example, Ted Kennedy, long time Senator, died last year – or was it the year before. Either way, here is a Senator who stole hundreds of millions of taxpayer dollars to feed his pet projects. But for some reason, when he died, he became a saint.

I've seen this happen over and over. Unless you are at the level of horribleness of Adolf Hitler or Saddam Hussein (and I'll bet there were even some who did not celebrate his demise, despite the millions he abused and killed) for some reason, even though these were horrible people in real life, stole, treated people terribly, they seem to become wonderful angels who should be remembered fondly

Why is this? Does someone become a better person in death? Does the fact that they can't turn themselves around and ask forgiveness for their sins from the people they made suffer suddenly make them better people? I don't think so.

Do people really become saints when they die? No. and if someone was horrible in life, they haven't changed once they die.

I guess it's a left over from when we figured if you said bad things about dead people, they might come back to haunt you. I think we all know that's not true.

Unless it is, in which case just take everything back that I just said.

Capitalism = Evolution

Back in 1990, I read Bionomics: Economy as Ecosystem, an excellent book by Michael Rothschild. Very eye opening and a very important read for anyone who has any question at all that capitalism is the only system which works for the human race. Go get it on Amazon right now; I just checked you can get a paperback copy for $0.07 plus $4 shipping.

Got it yet? No, I know I don't usually drop everything either when an author tells me to go do something right now. I think of all those self-help books with uncompleted worksheets in them that I sold on Amazon or at used bookstores, where the author specifically says "Stop reading now and fill out this form!"

Anyways, since you haven't read the book yet, let me give you the synopsis. The author looks at biology and evolution, something that most people now agree is no longer a theory but fact: sure some conservative Christians continue to believe in creationism, but I think most of you reading this book agree that evolution, either natural or initiated by some higher being, either God, Zeus or the Flying Spaghetti Monster, did probably occur and is probably occurring right now. So if you assume that evolution IS happening, then you think, what economic system will work with evolution, instead of against evolution. There is only one economic system which is nearly an exact match with evolution, and that is capitalism.

Think about nature. Do you really see socialism or communism in nature? Do you see large scale sharing, or animals working together to help each other, outside of small groups or families? No you don't.

My argument is that any other economic system is basically unnatural. Our genetic makeup is geared to capitalism and the free market. Anything else is trying to go against human nature.

Ah but of course, many of the socialists out there say that well, then human nature is wrong. We are trying to make the human race better. We are trying to improve it beyond its base tendencies. But the problem is always there. It's almost impossible to change the nature of a species. Even those who are in power, and truly believe in the socialist mindset, never truly see everyone as equal, or that the rich should enjoy the same benefits as the poor. There is no equality is socialism, only stated. In reality, there is no such thing as a fair system. It does not and cannot exist.

So why fight evolution and human nature? Why go against the grain by doing things like not keeping score at your kid's soccer game? Or letting schools go up against each other by implementing school vouchers? We should just embrace our inner capitalist and let it out! Why do you think China, Russia and India are eating our economic lunch?

They get it.

Historic

OMG. If I never hear the word "historic" again in my whole life I may just about be happy.

Ever since our Savior, the anointed one Barack Hussein Obama, ascending to the holy office of Emperor of the United States, seems like everything this guy does is labelled historic, simply due to the fact that this guy is multiracial. It's almost like history began when this guy entered office.

1. Historic Election
2. Historic Win
3. Historic Presidency
4. Historic Meetings
5. Historic First Press Conference

Blah. Blah. Blah. I wonder if the media covered the Savior's first crap in the White House. Yes, folks, it was a historic day when the winner of the historic election took office in this historic year and had his first historic visit to the historic restroom in the historic West Wing.

If you ask me, there is nothing even remotely historic about the Obama election OR presidency, unless you factor in the race card. I mean, it's true, isn't it? I'm not being racist, I'm just stating fact. If Obama were white, instead of half white, what would be the "historic" significance of his election? Absolutely nothing. Would the media be saying "historic" if it was, say, John Edwards, instead of Barack Obama? Did the media use the word "historic" when John

Kerry ran against Bush in 2004? Nope. So the only way you can consider this election or presidency "historic" is if you ARE racist. Think about that for a second. Everyone using the word "historic" is being a racist. How does that make you feel about the media using that word?

And even now, two years on, where he campaigned on a platform of "hope" and "change", which some thought was bi-partisan and "transformative", none of that has come to pass. Obama turned out to be a new fresh wrapper for the same old socialist ideals which have been proven to be the "failed policies of the past". There's nothing historic about a slick politician fooling the American people into thinking that they represent real change.

Like that hasn't happened a million times before.

Augmenting Humanity

So, Mother Nature, God or whoever got us to this point in history. If you believe in God, he set us down on this Earth for a reason. If you believe in evolution, you must feel that we must continue to improve ourselves.

So this is what I think. I think that the reason we discovered genetic manipulation, including the ability to re-write our genetic code in order to strip out diseases, create blond haired, blue eyed babies, or even dark haired, brown eyed babies, or any variation of the above, was that we were destined, either by God or Nature, or augment ourselves. That the next step of human evolution, or ascension, is human driven.

To the believers: Why did God give us the knowledge to manipulate future generations unless He wanted us to do it?

To the evolutionists: Isn't it possible that the reason we know how to evolve ourselves now is because we evolved the knowledge to evolve ourselves?

So either way: we have gained the knowledge to improve ourselves, and our progeny greatly. If we truly are to expand the human race to its fullest potential, we should use any and all methods, including genetic manipulation, cloning and drugs in order to improve the human race. And in the search for this improvement, we have to stop saying "should we" and start saying "we must!"

Now some of you are saying, boy, this sounds an awful lot like Hitler, eugenics etc. What is to stop the rich from creating armies of blond-haired, blue-eyed babies, and breeding everything else out? Well, I'm for the complete, widespread adoption of these technologies, to the point that everyone, of any flavor of humanity, can create their progeny in their own image, or whatever image that like. I think that there is no shortage of potential parents out there who would not wish for disease free children.

So let's stop holding ourselves back, and see what the human race can really do when it sets its mind on it.

Sarah Louise Palin

I just don't really get the hubbub surrounding Sarah Palin. If you ask me, she is also a YAP, Yet Another Politician, simply using her personal persona to get ahead. She may be "Aw Shucks you betcha" on the surface, but in reality she is just as cold and calculating as Obama and the rest of them.

When she first appeared on the scene, although I did hear that there were rumors of her being a possible VP candidate with Ron Paul, there was an incredible commotion on both sides – some thought "what the hell is McCain doing – is he looking to throw the election?" or the exact opposite "this is exactly what the GOP needed a sexy shot in the arm"

Even I was drawn in by this strange attractor. I did a cursory search against her policies and stands on things and found them interesting, mostly anti-big government, but her strong social conservatism turned me off. Still it made the 2008 election interesting.

I tell you though: I just don't get it. What is the appeal of Sarah Palin? She seems to elicit pure love or hate in most people – but like I said, I think most people don't see her as yet another politician.

Think about when she quit the governorship. The media portrayed it as either a really dumb move that would take her out of the limelight, or a really shrewd move that would help her develop a stronger independent grass roots effort. Hardly anyone mentioned that it was mostly due to saving the state and herself a ton of cash fighting frivolous lawsuits brought against her by the aforementioned haters.

So I thought: is she really in love with her political beliefs, or as a YAP, willing to change her spots in order to win the Presidency? If she truly is a YAP, then maybe she SHOULD hook up with Ron Paul / Rand Paul, or someone else in a Campaign for Freedom style movement. Maybe the exact shot in the arm we need is to couple the policies of Ron Paul with the mouthpiece of Sarah Palin. I even did a show on this at one point. What if we could turn Sarah Palin into a living, breathing bullhorn for freedom?!

Ok, so maybe it's a bad idea. But we certainly need something more than Tea Parties and other such similar protests, when even 2 million protesters march on Washington and no one hears anything. The media is so in bed with the Obama administration and their policies, maybe we need something even more radical. I'd be willing to hold my nose and use Sarah Palin to further the cause of liberty, as long as she is willing to change her views to mimic ours.

Sarah Palin 2012? Don't shoot me, but what if the choice in 2012 was between Sarah Palin and Barack Obama? Would I vote for Palin? You betcha!

Lesser of two evils, again.

Nobel Peace Prize

The biggest scam this side of global warming. Tell me how any of these people contributed to PEACE:

1. Woodrow Wilson
2. Neville Chamberlain
3. Henry Kissinger
4. Anwar Sadat
5. Mikhail Gorbachev
6. Yasser Arafat
7. Kofi Annan
8. Jimmy Carter
9. Al Gore
10. Barack Hussein Obama

I don't think can say anyone on this list doesn't have some blood on their hands. And they get a prize for peace? Is that like getting a "most improved student" prize. Sure, I used to send troops to their deaths, but I'm much better now and deserve a Peace Prize. What the hell does Al Gore and his wacko, kooky environmentalist nutcase cult have anything to do with peace?

And Barack Hussein Obama got his before he did a damn thing. In fact, one could argue that it took him longer to make the decision to send more troops into Afghanistan in order to shorten the conflict there simply because he won the Nobel Peace Prize. He was probably up one night thinking after his generals had told him that the situation in Afghanistan was getting worse and worse since the coalition over there wasn't doing a very good job of making things better over there, and that more troops and civilians were dying EVERY day if he didn't take some action to send more troops over there in a similar surge to Iraq's (which to this day he believes did not help even though there are facts that state that it clearly did). So he is up one night pondering having to send more American troops into battle in order to turn things around, and he is ready to make the decision to go ahead, thus turning things around sooner and saving countless lives. The next morning he gets a call from the Nobel committee telling him that he just won the prize. Immediately he calls a meeting with his closest advisors (Let's call them the Chicago Gang):

Obama: Dudes, you know things in Afghanistan are getting worse

CG: Yeah we know.

Obama: You know I was just about to send more troops over there to fix things

CG: Yeah, remember we suggested that too. Just don't call it a surge.

Obama: Got it. But there's a wrinkle, just came up.

CG: What is it?

Obama: The f-ing Nobel Peace Prize people just called and gave me the prize.

CG: S**t, man, no way.

Obama: Way.

CG: Well, you can't send any troops now, man that would look really bad.

Obama: I know. WTF do I do now?

CG: Well, you can't send more troops RIGHT AFTER being awarded the prize. So why not just wait for a bit. We can spin it that this is a very difficult decision for you and you are weighing all the options before you decide to put more people in harm's way blah blah. We'll monitor the chatter and let you know when it's OK to go ahead and give the go-ahead.

Obama: Sounds good.

CG: (One of the Gang has a bit of a conscience) Of course, that means that the situation will get worse while you are delaying. Isn't that bad too?

Obama: Sure, but the media don't care that much about Afghan civilians and a few of our troops dying. Not as important as me looking bad. Know what I mean?

You were here. You saw what happened. Right after Obama won the prize, there were all these photos and stories showing him looking very pensive and troubled – should he send troops – should he not – if so how many – this went on and on and on – even the Generals in the region where starting to get so worried that they started their own information offensive in the media in order to try and get him to hurry up and make a decision. Am I wrong? Maybe, but don't you think that its possibly that a YAP like Obama is so wrapped up in his personal image and brand that he'd prefer to let unknown Afghanis and troops die just so that he doesn't look bad?

I mean, kings and queens have been doing it for centuries, haven't they?

The liege is much more important than the peasants.

Ethics Schmethics

This is really annoying to me.

I went to a seminar once on "life extension". But it wasn't a typical seminar on life extension, where you'd think people would be talking about ways in the ways in which to extend one's life.

No, it was about the ethics of life extension. They were not asking the question "Can we extend our lifespan to 100, 200, 300 years" it was "should we?"

Now, I was kind of taken aback by that. I couldn't understand why anyone would NOT want to live a longer life. But there it was: two opposing viewpoints on IF we should even try to extend our lives not how.

The Pro guy was very good. He was a leader in the field of life extension. He started explaining that a lot of the people who didn't like the idea probably figured that it couldn't be done. He explained one theory that like Moore's Law of computer power doubling every year, all we needed to do was to extend our life spans by 20 years, because within those 20 years we'd figure out how to extend it another 20, and so on. It was very exciting to me to hear this.

The Con guy was also very good, but he seemed very – pessimistic. He started asking why we should even try to live a longer life, how that would basically wreck our society, how everything has a season, blah, blah, blah. His whole argument was that life would be too different in a world where people lived to 300. He was basically saying: "Don't even bother trying"

So this is the thing that really bugs me, and this is only one example.

Why are there so many so-called "ethicists" out there telling us NOT to even try something, even if we don't know that it is even possible?

I mean, that goes against every rule of science that I know of. In fact, isn't it true that the only way science has been able to progress over the course of time is that we DID put ethics and morality aside in the name of scientific progress and in so doing invented and discovered so many things we never would have?

It seems like, to me, in the biological science space, we no longer just explore all of the possible permutations of some solution, but purposely question our motives ahead of time, thus stifling promising research.

I read somewhere that researchers were having trouble getting a release to experiment on fleas. And this is for a human virus vaccine. Please.

The only way science and the human race can progress is if we suspend ethics in the name of scientific inquiry.

Barack Hussein Obama AKA The "Savior"

I like to call Barack Hussein Obama "The Savior" Of course you can't hear me say it in this book, but it's kind of like the way a preacher in a Gospel church might say it – The Saaaaaaaavvvveeeeeooor! Nice little flourishes at the end. And yes, many people believed that he was all that: Jesus, God and the Holy Spirit, come to this world to save us. To bring us "hope". To "Change" things. You can see it in the imagery around the election. There were many depictions of Obama as holy, with halos, even the media had this habit of photographing him with his logo over his head, behind his head, intimating a halo or a religious connotation. You can see it in a ton of Flickr photos: just go to Flickr and search for "change". Almost 90% of what you will see there is photos of Obama, or of his followers. Truly, I think this was the first time in a long time that the American people were fooled into thinking this guy was the greatest.

Recently, I did an episode of my radio show called "Obama: It's a word that makes white people smile". This was a riff on an episode of a show I enjoy (now sadly cancelled I think) called Better Off Ted. In that show, they did fake commercials for the fictional company which all of the characters on that show work for, Veridian Dynamics. In one commercial, the tag line was "Diversity: it's a word that makes white people smile". It's true. One of the main reasons people thought Obama was so great was the fact that people could vote for him thinking that they had salved some great issue of conscience – that simply electing an African-American to the post of President would solve all of our problems, show the rest of the world how progressive we are, and change the face of the world as we know it.

You know, Obama didn't used to be so annoying. Back in 2004, when he appeared on the stage at the Democratic National Convention, he said some interesting things:

Tonight, we gather to affirm the greatness of our nation -- not because of the height of our skyscrapers, or the power of our military, or the size of our economy. Our pride is based on a very simple premise, summed up in a declaration made over two hundred years ago:

We hold these truths to be self-evident, that all men are created equal, that they are endowed by their creator with certain inalienable rights, that among these are life, liberty and the pursuit of happiness.

That is the true genius of America, a faith -- a faith in simple dreams, an insistence on small miracles; that we can tuck in our children at night and know that they are fed and clothed and safe from harm; that we can say what we think, write what we think, without hearing a sudden knock on the door; that we can have an idea and start our own business without paying a bribe; that we can participate in the political process without fear of retribution, and that our votes will be counted -- at least most of the time.

And:

...There is not a liberal America and a conservative America -- there is the United States of America. There is

not a black America and a white America and Latino America and Asian America -- there's the United States of America.

These are simply some selections from his speech there. There are others but these really stand out for me, since they are so in conflict with his positions of today. For example, do you recall the systematic suppression of any speech which the Obama campaign and administration felt was critical to him? So much for being able to say what we think.

And for the second quote, I think this is where he went the most wrong. If you think about it, he could have been the perfect candidate: if he truly believed in what he said back in 2004, his background positioned him perfectly as the candidate who could truly be post-racial – of course we couldn't know at the time how there was no way that he could be post-partisan. But there was an expectation that he could be something different.

Alas, it was not meant to be. Obama turned out, as most of them do, to be Yet Another Politician. I wonder what all these people are doing now:

1. With an Obama bumper sticker
2. Wrote and sang songs about Obama
3. Wrote children's books about Obama
4. Portrayed Obama as a superhero, saving the world
5. Those who spent a ton of money and time on his campaign
6. Those who named a school after him almost the moment he won the election, without

even seeing what kind of president he would be.

7. Those who named their children Barack. Funny, I thought only suppressive states like Iraq or North Korea named their children after their Dear Leaders

8. Those anti-war activists who see him send a ton more troops overseas

9. Those libertarians who voted for him expecting him to pull us out of all countries overseas

10. Those people from other countries who cheered him on during the election now watching him completely ignore and disrespect their own countries and their leaders

11. Those people who watched him bail out the banks and flood their executives with cash

12. Him turn an about face on card check

13. Being anything but transparent on things

14. Believed in him. Remember that quote from someone during that campaign that "Barack will pay for my gas and mortgage". How many people have been kicked out of their homes, lost their jobs and have had their utilities shut off since the Savior has been in office.

There are many, many, many more examples:

1. Closes Guantanamo Bay, has no plan for placing the inmates

2. Practically declares War on Capitalism, Cheerios and fast food
3. Calls detractors "racist"
4. Embraces enemies, shuns allies
5. Surrenders to terrorism
6. Hope turns to Fear when we wants something done
7. Continues government takeover of our lives, started by Bush & others before him
8. Dines on $100 a pound Wagyu Steak while country burns
9. Plays golf more times in his first year than Bush in both terms
10. Brings Chicago thug politics to the national level
11. Pushes $787B stimulus bill, touts bill will save economy, does not…
12. Compares his bowling skills with that of handicapped children.
13. Budget exceeds $3T dollars, yet thinks he's a budget cutter when he asks for $100M in savings
14. Bows deeply to Saudi prince, Japanese emperor, and others
15. Cap & Trade a huge tax on everyone
16. Stimulus turns out to be patronage for Obama's buddies
17. Tells wounded GIs to pay for their own treatment
18. Stimulus bill gives huge bank bonuses
19. Unemployment keeps going up, despite the stimulus bill

20. Elections held in Iran. Government bloodily suppresses protests against obvious fraud. Obama REFUSES to take sides. Only a tyrant won't take sides against tyranny
21. Talks wage and price controls
22. Talks warrantless search and seizure
23. Sings kumbaya against nuclear missiles
24. Says America is not a Christian nation
25. Obama reveals military secrets
26. Hugs fellow tyrant Hugo Chavez
27. Forces Swiss to reveal accounts. No rest from tyrannical, greedy governments
28. Buzzes NYC for a photo op. Millions freaked out
29. Business starts to live in fear of Washington
30. Auto industry fails, gets bailed out by taxpayers. But still – no one gets a free car. Creates a $1300 car tax
31. Michelle hugs the Queen – why not their all royalty now, right?
32. Releases Iranian terrorists right after 75 killed in Baghdad bombings
33. Shills for the 2016 Olympics in Chicago
34. Suggests we invite Iranians for July 4th BBQ
35. Pays off $11M per Gitmo prisoner
36. Talks directly to school kids, no parents allowed
37. Makes the same mistakes which extended the depression
38. Rams through 3 trillion dollar health care bill, destined to destroy not only our finances, but the sovereignty we have over our own bodies and burdening our culture for generations

39. Snitches on Arizona to the United Nations human rights commission.
40. Allows racism cases against white people to drop – so much for the post racial presidency
41. Parties on the beach in the south of France – or was that just Michelle and the princesses? Either way, its a shameful thing to be doing while the country is suffering from the worst depression since the Great Depression. To add insult to injury, is it precisely the actions of this administration, and the one before it – which caused this depression in the first place (This is why I like to call it the Bobama Depression, since while the Bush administration started it, the Obama administration helped to extend it and make it worse, payola to all of his cronies for helping him win the election in the guise of a "stimulus" bill)
42. Parties with his buddies, while Egypt roils in revolution

This could be a whole book. Actually I think a few people out there have written at length. Just remember people: Obama, and ANY POLITICIAN for that matter, is the Savior. We are the saviors, my friends. It is the American people who will save us: not Barack Obama, not Sarah Palin, not Scott Brown, not Mitt Romney.

You and I. We will save America. We just need the state to get out of the way. Don't lead or follow.

Just get out of our way.

Evolution

As I mentioned, I believe in evolution. Whether you believe that evolution happened naturally, or that some Supreme Being – or maybe even not so supreme – (could have been aliens right?) – kicked off our evolutionary process, I think most people can safely say that evolution has happened and continued to happen.

Thanks Mother Nature, or whoever, for taking us this far. It is now time for us to take over.

What do I mean by that? Simple. Why should we wait for natural selection and evolution to augment the human race, when we now have the capability to do it ourselves? We now have the capability to genetically engineer ourselves to be better. To erase diseases from our future progeny. To create better humans. To augment ourselves biologically, or mechanically.

Everyone I know has a cell phone, smart phone, or other such device. One can argue that we are already cyborgs that we need this technology in order to survive in the world that we currently live in.

You are probably wondering, Future, why are you bringing this up? Well, like I mentioned before, I'm constantly being compared to these right wingers who feel that every single forward movement is threat. That we should revert back to earlier centuries, or think really hard before we do anything to make the human race better. There are detractors on both sides, actually, people who like to sit and question and navel gaze about the future of the human race.

Well, my friend, the future is ours for the taking. We can decide ourselves; we have the technology, so to speak, in order to make ourselves a better race. The question is will we use that, or will we simply relegate it because we don't know what the effects may be?

This is not how we progress. This is not how we move forward. Innovation requires risk. Do you think that the inventors of flight put their safety above learning how to fly? Or the inventors of the car or the light bulb. Invention, progress, all requires risk and a leap of faith.

The greatest discoveries of humankind come from someone somewhere saying "What if..." then DOING IT.

Legalize Drugs Now

Here's another thing I say which annoys those on the right who listen to my show or read my stuff. I believe in complete legalization of every illegal drug that's out there. That's right. Complete and total legalization. Has to be better than what is going on right now on the War on Drugs

First:

1. Legalize everything: and I mean everything from pot to hash to coke to crack. Steroids too.
2. Just like selling smokes or liquor, you'd need a license, but you can apply just like anyone else
3. Open up the prisons and let the drug dealers and possessors out
4. Let drugs into the country the same way that any other product enters the country
5. Tax 'em, just like you tax any other business.

Simple eh? Too radical for most folks to understand. Do you know why so many lives and so much money has been lost on this front? The War on Drugs is much worse than the drugs themselves. It's the scarcity and the illegality which drives up the prices to where people will gladly kill to make money off this thing. If you read my nugget on Sin Taxes, a ton of violence was completely alleviated in Canada by reducing the hefty taxes on cigarettes.

You do the same thing for drugs here – you completely undermine the market. Drugs become cheap and plentiful. And sure, it may lead to a minor increase – but you have to trust in the ability and responsibility of individuals to refrain from taking them.

And even if people do start doing more drugs, they are totally completely and utterly responsible for themselves.

Some of you are crying out: "what about the children?" Keep them out of their hands the same way we keep smokes and booze out of their hands. Sure they can still get them – but it's up to you – the parents – to instill the proper values in these kids so that they can understand how harmful these things can be.

I for one and sick and tired for taking care of people who should be taking care of themselves. People are adults; we should start treating them that way – letting them make their own decisions.

OK, so let's try an experiment. Start with pot. Legalize it first, let it get established and then start on the rest. At least we will have done something constructive about the problem instead of just throwing people in jail. It's been proven that that doesn't work. So listen up, Mr. Savior, why don't you do something about this?

Show us that you really are for true "change"

We Are A Pimple on Mother Nature's Ass

Ah yes. Mother Nature. As I write this, there has been a quake in Chile. A tsunami may be headed for Japan and other Pacific islands. A few weeks ago there was a devastating earthquake in Haiti. The Northeast of the US has been hit with horrible storms. Remember the tsunami in Indonesia? Hurricanes in Florida. Or Katrina/Rita hitting the Gulf Coast. And according to Al Gore and his cadre of wackos, it's all humanity's fault. It's us driving cars and eating burgers that's causing all of this. So wrong.

Face it people. It's a pure question of scale. We are simply a pimple on Mother Nature's Ass.

There is a great joke about this in the Hitchhikers Guide to the Galaxy which illustrates what I mean. There is one section where they talk about an alien race getting ready to invade the planet Earth. They prepare these massive armies, build thousands of starships, then fly many light years across the galaxy in order to launch a massive invasion of Earth.

"However due to an error in scale the whole force was wiped out when a dog yawned and swallowed the lot"

It is the environmentalists who are making a similar error. You see, I firmly believe that whatever we do, excepting of course for say, a global thermonuclear war, where every nuclear country unloads their missiles on each other, the Earth can take pretty much everything we throw at it.

Why? Scale again. Imagine a million ants attempting to move your house. No matter how many ants you throw at the house, there is no way that house will move. Sure, they may make some inroads in undermining the foundation, and possibly eat up some of the timber, but no matter how many ants try to move bits of house, the scale of the house is just too massive. That's exactly what we are like against the might of this planet. It could fart and wipe us all out in a minute.

The earth is similar: yes we swarm over it. And yes, in some areas, we may make inroads where the Earth is scarred. But overall, we aren't ever going to see a man-made cataclysmic event, ala 2012. Not going to happen.

The Earth is not a static entity: it is a living thing. Not only is it a living thing, it's a thing that can bounce back from adversity. Think about it: the Earth has been through a hell of a lot more than we puny humans can throw at it, and it survives.

So unless we get really stupid and start throwing around a ton of nuclear missiles at each other, then I think you can be safe in using that incandescent bulb, running your hot water heater hot, chopping down trees on your property, and driving everywhere using up fossil fuels. Course you may not want to do that since the government will tax you up the ying-yang in order to address this false premise.

Trust me, the Earth can take it.

Man Is Part of the Planet

Another thing that bugs me about these Earth first people, environmentalists and the Al Gore quacks is that they somehow believe that man is some weird invading alien force which has somehow landing on this planet from somewhere else and is now systematically tearing the planet apart so we can take it over. We are not an invading alien force that needs to be repelled. We are part of this planet, in fact we are the masters of this planet, and should consider ourselves just that. What's wrong with that? If you believe in God, then He put us at the top of the food chain. If you believe in evolution, then we evolved to be there. Either way, that is where we are, that is where we are meant to be, and that is where we should stay.

Take the term "overpopulation". I mean, what exactly does that mean? Too many people? How can you actually say that there are "too many people". If you ask me, there are as many people are there are. Only someone who believes that the human race is a blight on the planet can possibly believe in "overpopulation"

I often wonder why if someone is so concerned about overpopulation they don't simply kill themselves in order to help to solve this problem. I think one less idiot might actually help. Just kidding, of course.

The human race is here, and it's here to stay. Therefore, we have to simply understand that we need to make room for humanity. In reality, there is plenty of space and food for everyone.

In the past, many pundits have predicted the end of the world being nigh if we simply hit some kind of milestone: whether it's the year 1000, 2000, 2012, 5 billion people, 6 billion people, 7 billion people etc. Every time one of these pundits makes a prediction about the demise of the human race, they are wrong. The human race survives. We are designed to survive. In fact, left alone, without intervention of the state, we survive even better.

Do you remember when the pundits predicted widespread famine and the human race dying off? Well, other humans invented new ways of creating more food, and suddenly, humanity survives.

Do you know the major reason why there is so much famine in the world? Why there is still so much suffering in many places around the globe? It's not because there are too many people. It's because there is too much government. I'll bet that if you zoom in on any hotspot around the globe where things are horrific for people, it's due to some government action or another.

The reality is that humans are a part of the world. And we should not just accept that, we should revel in it. There is something special about humanity, and everything we do and create.

I mean, don't you ever look around at everything around you and think, man, humans created all this. The desk you are sitting at, the room around you, the house you are sitting in, the town you live in, the roads in and out, the airplanes to and from up to the satellites circling. All invented in the inventive brain of a human being.

We truly are pretty awesome.

Global Vagueness

So this is the last I'll say on the whole global warming/cooling/climate change thing-me-bobber.

I was going to talk about how they all started talking about global warming, so that they changed the "brand" to "climate change" so they could blame any weather pattern on this. I was going to talk about how really we are so puny in comparison to the Earth that we couldn't really affect it. I had a lot of evidence that it was all a scam, simply yet another scam to extract millions of dollars out of our pockets and reduce our freedoms, something the state seems to love doing.

I had a whole big giant chapter on this but then it went and exploded. Some of the people perpetrating this scam actually felt some real remorse for ripping off the world so badly and made public that fact that a lot of the data was "manipulated" in order to give the results they wanted.

Boo-hoo. I can't believe people were sucked in by this scam. But it's their own fault.

Reminds me of a guy I saw at a "ethics of life extension" thing I went to. This guy, during one point when questions were being asked, stood up and started talking about how he wanted to extend his life because he had devoted most of it so far to helping to save the planet and avert climate change, which he felt was so important that he completely threw his whole life into it and therefore had no job, no life, no relationships with anyone. He had totally thrown himself into the activist role to the exclusion of all else. I wonder how this guy feels now, that everything he had worked for was a lie. Then I realized that people like that can never accept the truth. Someone like that could never see things a different way. He had checked his "reason" out at the door and never questioned anything that he was doing.

I KNEW it was all a scam from the beginning.

Symbolism Uber Alles

Something about many progressives and liberals that really bugs me. It's the fact that they seem to prefer symbolism and spreading awareness about something rather than actually doing anything about it.

I first remember seeing that when I used to have to watch the Academy Awards for my job. I remember

it was just around the time AIDS was making its way to America. There was a wash of all of these actors wearing a red ribbon, in "solidarity" or helping to "raise awareness" for AIDS. I thought, what exactly is the point? What are they actually DOING? I guess wearing a red ribbon is preferable to actually personally volunteering at an AIDS hospice or donating a ton of their own money towards the cause.

That reminds me of another thing. Why is it that whenever these rich celebrities get together to support a cause, they don't do it with their OWN money? How come we never see celebrities announcing that they are going to donate some of their copious wealth to the cause of the day, only that they give up their own time so that they can get their fans to pull out their wallets. Sure there are a few celebrities who just open their wallets and give to causes, Mel Gibson being one example, without expecting their fans to give it up for them.

Think about it. Ever since "We Are The World" rich celebrities have been getting together to record songs or do concerts or whatever, simply to extract money out of our wallets for some cause that they believe in. They are all already incredibly rich. Why don't they just open their OWN wallets and throw some cash where they believe it should go.

But I digress. Symbolism is so much easier than actually doing the work. If I wanted to help someone, I would actually do it, or open my wallet and donate. I wouldn't wear a pin that says "I donated". Anyone can do that. Anyone can say that they support something. It's the ones who actually take action and don't crow about it – those are the real heroes.

The symbolism goes far beyond celebrities and charities though. Politicians, especially leftist progressives, somehow think that making these gestures actually makes a real difference. That somehow, a gesture is all that's required in order to change the way things go.

That's not the real world. I can tell you that I believe in something until I'm blue in the face, but unless I take action, then what is my word worth. Obama can write up an order closing Guantanamo Bay, or make a statement of support for an insurgency inside Iran, but without actual backing, why bother? Why do you think the rest of the world doesn't take Obama seriously anymore? All talk, no action.

Bush, with all his faults, eventually did take action, for better or worse.

Take Heed, Republicans

Take heed, Republicans. If you ever want to get back into power, you need to be more conservative and libertarian. Ever wonder why those polls saying the country is on the wrong track DON'T CHANGE no matter who is in power? It's because NEITHER party is the party of the people. NEITHER party wants to go back to the founder's vision of America. But the American people DO.

The fact is, people are starting to wake up to the fact that we only really have one political party in this country. Well, for those true believers, lets say will still have two. But you know what those two are?

Socialist and Socialist Lite. I bet that you can guess which one is which.

I mean come on people: even McCain was pushing for socialized medicine. That's not a true conservative or even libertarian or even anything-based-on-the-founders party stance.

So, as I pen this (well, type it on my awesome Ubuntu laptop, actually) the GOP is ready to come back roaring since none of Obama's policies have turned things around in this country. (And really were we that stupid that we expected them to?) They are rubbing their hands together with delight, seeing how the American people are fed up with the leftist policies of Obama. Yes, they didn't want Bush, or McCain, but they didn't want this as well.

Of course, they are playing the "true conservative" card, some, even Glenn Beck, have actually come out and said "I'm more of a libertarian than a conservative"

To that I say: HAH!

Don't be fooled, people. These people are all still YAPs – all they care about is getting elected. Remember: use that thing that makes you human – your brain – look into the background of the politicians that you are about to elect: do they really believe in the founders vision? Are they really into moving America back to the constitution? Or are they just telling you that because they want to get elected?

If the GOP truly wants to be the party of the people, and stay in power for a really long time, the quickest way to do that is to truly DUMP any socialist lite tendencies within the party and fully embrace the libertarian agenda.

Will that happen? Doubtful. They'll probably take on some of the characteristics of the Tea Party and or libertarianism, then once they get in power, it'll be same-old same-old.

But until they do: or someone does: then things can only get worse and not better.

America, Disheartened

Obama and his ilk don't care if Americans are disheartened. They are ideologues through and through and only care about implementing their agenda. It doesn't matter what damage is done to the psyche of this country, as long as they get what they want.

You see, I'm generally an optimist, and I think that most Americans are optimists as well. I think they they understand that its part of the nature of America, sure we can make mistakes, and go down the wrong path for a while, but then we can turn things around and go down the right path

In the past, we were always able to see a future. Not this time.

When people are starting to be taxed 50,60, 70%+, they will give up - they are not automatons that will simply do the Saviors bidding.

Americans understand how important it is to support success, not penalize it.

Will this attitude of false optimism in our government kill America?

Actually, no. I some ways, I think Obama did us a huge favor. If you think about it it, in 2008, we had a choice between what we had - the Bushist neo-con style of politics - which is still pretty liberal - liberal lite I like to call it - and Obama - who represented change - but what kind of change we didn't really know at the time. So really, he did us a favor. By selecting Obama's rapid Road To Serfdom, as opposed to McCain's slow Road To Serfdom, people actually woke up and decided to take action against the encroachment of big government. If you think about it, the true progressives who really wanted to successfully shunt America to the left actually failed when they elected Obama – they would have had a better chance of solidly moving the country to the left had they stayed with the leftist light McCain.

Thinking short term ultimately killed the progressive movement, hopefully forever.

Why the Left Hates America

It's pretty simple actually. And you probably already know this.

America has always been about the people, not the state.

Whereas the left has already been about the state, not the people. The left cannot believe in people, not the state, as the solution. As far as they are concerned, the people are the idiotic unwashed masses who can barely understand how to get through a day, let alone do something as big and important as run a country! That's assuming that a country needs to be run.

You know, a lot of people, under a standard system of laws and rules, given freedom, will probably not turn into a mass of lawlessness. We proved that when this country was founded, and I bet we could even prove that today, that is if the government ever left us alone to prove it.

They are always there, the nanny state, making sure that we don't hurt ourselves or others.

We can run things ourselves. Sure, it may look a little chaotic, but it works, since we all know the rules (more or less) and we usually abide by them, and if we don't we had a pretty damn good system put in place to manage any of those who broke those rules. Of course, at some point, some people came along and, like the Kings and Queens before them, looked upon the little people of America and said: "someone needs to run this place"

America never needed to be "run" by anyone. America, from the beginning, was designed to be self-propelled, self-healing, and self-managed. All of those people, making decisions to "pursue life, liberty and happiness" in their own way, work just fine.

Read Adam Smith, The Invisible Hand:

By preferring the support of domestic to that of foreign industry, he intends only his own security; and by directing that industry in such a manner as its produce may be of the greatest value, he intends only his own gain, and he is in this, as in many other cases, led by an invisible hand to promote an end which was no part of his intention. Nor is it always the worse for the society that it was not part of it. By pursuing his own interest he frequently promotes that of the society more effectually than when he really intends to promote it. I have never known much good done by those who affected to trade for the public good. It is an affectation, indeed, not very common among merchants, and very few words need be employed in dissuading them from it.

And you know, I bet all of those busy-bodies in government who want to run everything actually know that things will run better, cheaper and more efficiently without their hands in the process. They just can't stand the thought of not controlling things and running other people's lives.

Remember, as libertarians, we let people live their lives, as long as they don't interfere with ours.

Steal Billions, Rebate Hundreds

Bush did this, and was laughed at. Obama did the exact same thing and was heralded as an economic savior. I wish someone would explain to me how stealing huge amounts of money from us, then returning a few pennies, helps us at all?

Remember Bush's big $300 refund checks, back after September 11th? How he figured all that he had to do was send out $300 checks to individuals and $600 checks to families and then all of a sudden the American economy would suddenly be back on track? At the time, everyone laughed at the concept. But then Obama did the exact same thing, and was lauded! Never mind the fact that the reaction to a specific event having anything to do with the party affiliation of the person in the office of the Presidency, how is that supposed to help?

Compare that measly $300 or $600 check with the thousands and thousands of dollars every level of government takes out of our pockets already. Go ahead, take out last year's W2, or go online and take a look at it. How many multiples of $300 or $600 is it? And it's not just that – think about the thousands and thousands of dollars in sales taxes you pay on almost everything, the thousands of dollars you have probably paid over time filling up your car in hidden fuel taxes, the taxes on your power, the taxes on your phone bill, the taxes on your cell phone bill, the taxes on your cable bill, the taxes on your Internet bill, on and on and on. We are taxed SO MUCH MORE than the measly rebate checks, one wonders if anyone up there has a brain at all, let alone any sense of economics.

It's high school economics, people.

Listen, Don't Speak

Obama's problem is that he doesn't listen. Surprising with those elephantine ears, isn't it. Well, dictators are not known to listen, are they?

Bush was the same way: remember the "Don't confuse me with facts, my minds made up" as he drove American troops to invade Iraq for no real, good reason.

One of the biggest issues which infects every politician (well, most) is their uncanny ability to be all ears BEFORE an election, going out amongst the people, holding focus groups, asking people what they want, what kind of leader they want them to be, etc. They go out of their way to be the people's friend, listening, learning, taking the people's concern to Washington, Sacramento (or the capital of your choice) or whatever. Before a politician is elected, they are all ears.

AFTERWARDS, of course, it's the exact opposite. Somehow their ears shrink to a vestigial size and no longer function. However, their mouths seem to grow even larger than their ears were before the election, as the turn around and tell us what to do. They tell us we don't understand how things work in Washington, Sacramento or the capital of your choice. They tell us that things are different from what they expected, that it will be much harder to implement the changes they promised, and that we would be lucky to even get a small portion of what we are asking.

In short, they stop listening and start telling. They start telling us what to do and how to think, like Jekyll and Hyde, being elected is some kind of magic transformative process which takes a decent, honest, listening individual and turns them into a mouthpiece for the state. Once they get elected, everything changes.

I'm not saying that all politicians are like that. But most are. They listen before, and only speak after. Funnily enough, in Obama's case, he never listened before the election either! But people were so sucked in by the "hope and change" message, were so tired of the "liberal light" Republican party, that they needed a change.

So, I'm not sure that we should be too surprised that he doesn't listen to the people now.

Being Rich Doesn't Have To Make You Annoying

Have you ever been up late at night and been sucked into watching those get rich quick schemes where you spend $X and you get all this stuff purporting to make you all this money. Proven systems blah blah blah. And you always seem to get these people going around and talking about how successful they are and what they did to succeed? Most of the time they are trying to sell you the same path to being successful that they took.

Problem is that the conditions for their success cannot be repeated, Otherwise we'd all be rich.

Being successful is a few things

1. Deciding what success is: are you looking at a million bucks in the bank, a house in Hawaii, or an awesome family life?
2. Going after what you think will lead you to success

There is no magic bullet. There is no free lunch. There is no way to make success pop out of nothing. Success depends on three things:

1. People
2. Place
3. Time

You need to connect with the right people, in the right place, at the right time. All of those things need to happen simultaneously for you to be successful. This is why all of these get rich schemes rarely work: they expect you to recreate the conditions under which they were successful, but there is NO WAY, barring the invention of a time machine, or better still a TARDIS, since you will need to be in the right place as well, you can recreate those conditions. The best you can hope for is to insert yourself into similar situations, and hope that lightning strikes twice. This is what most of these "success" books do: they basically tell the story of how the author got rich, but they really give no insight as to how you can get rich the same way, and if you think about it, its a double insult, since they just took your money and got richer telling you how they got rich, but not how you can get rich.

Additionally, like celebrities, some of these rich people think that their wealth is some kind of affirmation that what they have to say actually makes sense and has meaning, which is rarely the case.

I mean, look at Donald Trump.

Avatar Sucked

I tell you, there's not too many people on my "intensely dislike" list. A new addition is James Cameron, director of Terminator, Titanic, and now Avatar.

While James Cameron did a great job with the concept of the "Terminator" series, pretty much everything else is way downhill from there. I mean, if you look at Titanic, here is a guy who probably literally made billions from depicting the real suffering of others. I guess it was OK to make a movie about this tragedy and make a bundle at it, because it had happened so long ago. I wonder if the families of the victims of Titanic ever saw anything out of that. I'm wondering how long he is going to wait to do the same for 9/11.

But I digress. His latest flick, Avatar, if you ask me, is UNBELIEVABLY bad. I mean there is only one good thing about the movie: the visuals are amazing. You can say that the computer graphics teams went above and beyond the call of duty – you could say that Avatar was a triumph for programmers. An absolute triumph.

However, when it comes to everything else about the film, it stunk. The characters were simply cardboard cut-outs, the bad guys were bad guys, the good guys were good guys, there was absolutely NO character development whatsoever. I mean in real life, when a human being is presented with an ethical and moral choice, they usually ponder their situation and make a decision, they contemplate the consequences of their actions. Or if monumental events take place in their lives, it changes their perception of the world and they grow as a person.

We never saw any of that in Avatar. And not only did we not see any of that, we saw the same old, tired, liberal, socialist, elite version of the world, jammed in Cameron's (and pretty much every other Obama-Lovers) head. You know the drill:

1. Business people are bad. They always work to screw everyone over in the name of profits. To the point of killing their customers. (To this point, I hear that Oliver Stone, who made what was for me, one of the best movies of all time, Wall Street, was SO unhappy that people actually loved Gekko and wanted to pattern their lives after him and he has been itching to make a sequel where Gekko is SO much worse. Funny thing about socialists, they always seem surprised when sometimes people idolize the money-making bad guy. Not all of us have the same disdain for wealth that you do. In fact most of us strive for more of it – and at least we are honest when we say we want to be financially successful – you're the dishonest one, since you get financially successful by lecturing against it)

2. Military people are bad: they are glorify and enjoy making war. As far as I know, most military I know despise war. They know more than most of us the horrors of war, so if anyone was to hate war, it would be those closest to it. Sure there may be a few who got

in it for the fun of it – but those kinds of people are weeded out pretty fast. BTW, this hatred toward the military extends to our current administration.

3. Civilization is bad: we have lost touch with the natural world, and it is wrecking us. If it weren't for civilization, none of what we have would be here. Does he REALLY think that the world would be better off if we were all living in the jungle and wearing leaves? (God forbid we skin any animals for clothes) Maybe someone can remind Sir James that life was pretty harsh and short before civilization. These people who think that the world would be better off if we all rolled back to some pre-technical era are just deeply annoying.

4. Technology is bad: it has helped us to lose touch with the natural world. Uh, Cameron himself said that he had to wait until now to tell this story the way he did (Can't imagine why – I mean this same story has been told a million times since the time of Jesus – not sure why he had to wait for super-duper 3D technology to tell it one more time) – so he uses technology to tell a story about how bad technology is? I mean, for normal people, this is bizarre – but for some reason, these liberals can live with the incongruency – most of their lives are – do what I say, not what I do.

5. Natives are always good. Why is that? Why do they always portray these "noble" savages – when in reality that would kill without a

moment's thought? And it wasn't just to protect the tribe. This is where the word "savage" comes from, you know.

So, I'm really tired of the adulation for this film. And, I'm sure, its many sequels. But I'm not surprised. I mean, that ship has sailed long ago – I mean, when was the last time you remember of these scenes of a liberating soldier, greeted by cheers, instead of derision, or a businessman, lauded for simply making money and creating jobs, instead of donating money to build a safe house for children?

It's my hope that with the collapse of Hollywood, and the rise of inexpensive film technology, we will finally see some independent film making which promotes freedom, capitalism and business, instead of tearing it down.

Wouldn't that be great?

King of America

You know the presidency was never supposed to be like this.

In fact, politics, in general, are really only supposed to be part time jobs. Go back into the annals of history – you think the founding fathers were career politicians? No, they had much better things to do with their time than run other people's lives. Uh, wasn't that the whole idea behind America? When you make the assumption that people are basically good, and should be allowed to pretty much run their owns lives, then surprise, surprise, you end up with the freest, most prosperous nation on earth, (Don't tell Obama, he isn't too happy with us being the freest and most prosperous nation, that would mean that we are actually BETTER than all those other countries out there. Duh – why do you think people emigrate here in droves, as opposed to emigrating to say, Iraq.)

But I digress. The presidency, over the last 100 years or so, has gone from its humble beginnings as a part time job, simply the last checkpoint to confirm the will of the people, to a role as full of pomp, circumstance, and power – in fact, much much more power – a hundred, a thousand times worse than the regime we rebelled against, 200 odd years ago.

King George is child's play, compared to King Obama (or should I say Emperor Obama? But who is Obama's Darth Vader? Not Biden, he's more of a lower class C3PO. Now Cheney, he was an awesome Darth Vader). The enemy of free people, free speech and free markets is no longer across the pond, he is right there in the White House,

The old saw applies: power corrupts. As time passed, the presidency was given more and more power, successive administrations gave themselves more and more power, where I'd say that today, we are in worse shape than we were during the first American revolution. No man on earth has the level of power the president has, and we don't seem to really question giving him even more power.

Do we really need/want a new King and Queen to run our lives? Do people need that kind of authoritarian control over their lives? Have we really traveled so far away from our roots as to actively seek and install the same kind of royalty that we fled from?

It's funny how people originally from other countries, like myself, can totally see the parallels. For some odd reason, Americans seem to want to bring things that we fled from here, thinking that they are good things, like socialized medicine, social programs, and now having a "glamorous King and Queen" that we can look up to.

Politicians are not supposed to be royalty. Fleeing from royal impositions founded this country. And now we are trying to bring it back? One asks...why?

What do we miss so much about royalty that we keep wanting to return to it?

The Birth Certificate

Actually, this is a very interesting issue for me. Many of those out there who are asking about the birth certificate actually are doing it because they want to invalidate Obama's claim to the throne of America. I'm just curious.

I actually DON'T believe that being a natural born American should be a necessary qualification for the presidency. As an legal immigrant, I can tell you that there are plenty of immigrants who could be considered more American than natural born Americans. I mean these people really understand why America is the best place on Earth. They've lived elsewhere – they know and understand the differences. They deeply understand why America is the best place on Earth. And they are determined to keep it that way.

If you have not lived outside America, you take for granted the awesomeness of this country. You take for granted the opportunity you just don't have in these other countries. You take for granted the access to funding, the creative minds, the freedom to break out of your social caste, the ability to re-invent yourself, the ability to be amazingly successful or an incredible failure.

You take for granted that here, you can be who and what you want to be – that you won't be forced into living the life you were born into. As I mentioned in the Prozac nugget, America lets you be free to be the most incredible success, or the most amazing failure. America gives you the rope, you are the one to decide whether to use it to climb mountains, or to hang yourself.

So I feel that it's not necessary for the President to be born in America, only to have lived elsewhere during his/her life and understand why it is the best country on earth, and how to keep it that way.

Freedom on the March

If 2 million people show up and its makes no sound, what do you do? Then most recently 1 million for Glenn Beck's speech where MLK made his, and then a few weeks after that, a tepid response from the progressive community. I tell you, people are done with the Road To Serfdom.

I'm glad to be writing this. Over the last few years, ever since Obama was elected, I was concerned that the real core of America, the ability for it to correct itself when it did something really bad to itself, such as electing a full bore, America hating statist to the highest office in the land, as well as enough cronies to basically turn this republic into an oligarchy, was something which would irreparably damage America. For the last two years, ever since I went into the bunker, I've seen our free speech and free markets eroded like never before, I've seen open hatred of the markets which actually sustain all of this government activity, I've seen enormous government expansion, spending, and payoff to cronies. I've seen our debt rise to levels undreamed of, and a socialized medicine bill which is basically the last straw, finally breaking this country down to the point where it is no longer exceptional. A bill where we give up the last bastion – control over our own bodies – to the state.

One of the best things about America was its ability to correct itself after it has made a terrible mistake. I thought that was over – that we'd finally gotten to the point – like in many other countries – where the will of the people was finally broken to the point that we are basically too weary to correct things. I experienced that myself in Canada – the people want things to change – be better – but the will is gone. The government has so beaten down the people that they have lost the will to change.

I was worried that we were there as well. With all the talk of Obama saving the country, and paying for our gas and mortgage, I thought – that's it – we've succumbed to the entitlement society, and we are destined to complete our course down this path to utter banality, ala most European countries I know.

But then something happened. What happened was that Americans, sensing that things were going down the wrong path, began the correction process.

Its a wonderful thing. People waking up, leaving their jobs, becoming active. Doing something. Turning things around.

That's when you realize the big difference between America and pretty much every other country on the face of the planet. The people still run America. The people still have a say. And it's the people who will ultimately recreate the conditions.

It like that example I gave you earlier on about people butting into line ahead ot you. It's taken us a while, but we are finally saying: "the line ends back there, buddy"

In other countries, the people don't run the country. The politicians run the country, the people have willingly given up the rights to run the country, and pretty much allow the politicians to do whatever they like, thinking that they really have no choice in the matter.

No so here. That's what makes us so truly exceptional. WE still run the country, no matter what the government says. They still work for us, not the other way around. And it is this fundamental fact, which hopefully will never change.

And that is why we are exceptional.

Assholium or Unleashing Your Inner Asshole

Sometimes, the best thing you can be is a jerk.

Case in point. I used to work for a company which did professional services, we would sell a company a set of software, then we would consult with that company in order to install, launch and maintain this software at the company. When I started at this company, I was assigned to assist a project manager on a project in process. Apparently, the project was going a bit off track, they were burning hours and not a lot of things were going on. The PM in question was writing up plans and having meetings but things didn't seem to be happening.

The problem was, the guy was nice. Really nice. In fact, he was too nice. He was one of those guys who is great at getting things done when there was little to no resistance to his plans. But here there was a lot of resistance. So as the second-in-command here, I suggested that he bring out his "inner asshole" – basically, be a little tougher on them, and see what happens. When I first mentioned it to him, he was pretty apprehensive about it, I think he thought that it would get even worse and shut things down even more for him.

Funny thing though. He stood up to them and all of a sudden they backed down and fell in line. The project got back on the rails, and he went back to being a nice guy, but kept on the lookout just in case he needed to do it again.

Sometimes you need to be a jerk in order to get things done. You need to be a little more aggressive and assertive in order to accomplish a task, or gain respect.

It's similar to what's going on in the Middle East. Do you think that the terrorists who are using Islam to further their own ends respect America more or less since Obama stepped back and is being "nicer?" Do you think that America got more respect from these regimes now, or before when Bush was in power. When you are in a fight, sometimes you can be nice, but other times you have to bring out the big guns.

It's all about getting the job done, not about always being the nice guy. Sometimes you have to stoop down to someone's level in order to fight them. At least you can step back up, many times they can't. For example, let me give you my favorite Twilight Zone style example:

You wake up in a room, with 9 people. There are no doors and windows, no discernable way out.

You start to question the people in the room. You find that 8 of them are strict pacifists. However the 9th is a cold blooded killer, who would not hesitate to kill you all. Who comes out of that room alive?

You either have to use violence to subdue the murderer, or you will all be killed. For some of you extreme pacifists out there, that is an option. But in the end, the murderer will go free. Sometimes, as civilized men, we must stoop to the level of the barbarian in order to fight the barbarian.

And that, my friends, I learned from Star Trek, episode Mirror, Mirror.

Fanatics

When I was in university back in Canada, I took a class called Logic and Argument.

Now I loved this class, because most of it was devoted to discussion of the best way to argue a point.

As a pretty opinionated guy, I relished getting into discussions with my classmates. We had some really great discussions, on all sorts of topics.

My professor was a great guy. He taught me all about fanatics.

Now these "fanatics" as he called them, aren't the bomb-toting maniacs you possibly think that they might be. Sure, those guys ARE fanatics, but I'm talking about a different kind.

Sometimes, when you are in the middle of a discussion and debate, and you are trying to prove your point, you use a number of different techniques, and always use facts and objective measures in order to prove your point. At least you should if you are trying to make a reasoned argument for your point.

However, you my at some point get into a discussion where no matter what you say, no matter how much evidence you provide, no matter how well and logically you present your point, the guy on the other simply will not change his or her mind.

Don't confuse them with facts, their minds are made up.

My professor called these people "fanatics". He said that when you recognize that you are arguing with a fanatic, there is only one way out of the argument.

Walk away. You cannot change the mind of a fanatic. They do not listen to reason, fact and argument.

How many people in your life would you reckon are fanatics? How much time have you spent trying to convince them of something, using very logical, reasoned arguments, but still they don't budge?

Walk away.

I'll give you an example: I was talking to a co-worker one day about health care costs. It was his position that socialized health care was better since you did not have to pay for it. I countered with the fact that in countries with socialized health care, in some cases, life saving treatments are delayed due to state rationing in order to cut costs. So I said, what would you prefer, paying $40,000 to get a life saving treatment today, or waiting 6 months to get it for free, but you may die at any time within those 6 months without treatment. So I thought, seems like a reasonable option: if you could pay any price to keep from dying, then wouldn't you, if you could. He said "I'd prefer to die, then be in that much debt". How can you argue a point with someone who takes a completely illogical point of view?

You can't. Just walk away.

Givers and Takers

I have a dream. We all have a dream. And all the takers want is to tear that dream away from us. To feed themselves. To support themselves. Our dreams are not for us alone - our dreams help everyone. They do not care about anyone but themselves. We do - we care about rebuilding our world in such a way that everyone benefits. They only want to twist the world so that they benefit. The culture of entitlement we have created has been our undoing. We need to dismantle this. We need to change things so that the human parasites, the human diseases, the human vampires who infest this world will need to start being human. They will need to produce. They will need to learn to give.

They have the capacity to give. They can give enough so that they can fool the givers into giving them more. They can choose to give. If we can dismantle the culture of entitlement, then it won't be OK to glide through life on other peoples coattails. Maybe instead of the soccer moms complaining about how stupid their husbands are when they get together they talk about how their husbands contribute to their relationship. Maybe instead of talking about how they tried to work but found it overrated they exchange job seeking tips and ways in which to contribute to their relationships. Maybe then the divorce rate wouldn't be as high as it is. Maybe if couples and families worked as a team against the elements attempting to tear down the family - the family would still be together. Maybe if we didn't throw our kids out the door at 18 and told them to fend for themselves there would be less mall shootings. We built this culture over time, and it will take time to tear it down.

It's up to us to change the world for our children and theirs.

Ron Paul

I have a bone to pick with Doctor Paul. While I'm in complete agreement with his politics, he kinda screwed us over back in 2008.

The good doctor left us at the altar.

The Paulians shriek! "What are you talking about, Future? Dr. Paul has always furthered the cause of liberty his whole life. What could he have done differently"

Well, I'll tell ya. Cast your mind back to the 2008 election. There were a lot of Ron Paul supporters in that election. I even went out and canvassed for the man. I recorded interviews with the other canvassers as well, and featured them prominently on my show. I did whatever I could to support and promote him, because until that moment, I had never had anyone to vote for, just a lot of people to vote against.

In every previous election, I always had to vote for the lesser of the two evils (or three or four evils) in front of me at the ballot box. I had to hold my nose and vote for the least worst candidate. For the first time ever I thought: I can finally vote for someone instead of against someone else.

So I was enthralled by his vision – the fact that this guy really got it – and I wasn't the only one – there were millions of us – a sizeable voting block I would say – that agreed with his vision. Not just Republicans or Democrats or Independents, I could argue that his message resonated very strongly with all of us at some level (assuming that we are all libertarians, right?) When I went canvassing, many of the people I came across said "I believe in Ron Paul, I agree with what he stands for, but he can't win". So a lot of people voted for the candidate that they through would win instead of with their minds. Fair enough, but I digress.

So he didn't win the primary, but he still had a ton of supporters, from every side, who believed in his vision. I thought, this is great – he can galvanize all of the supporters who believe in him, all he has to do is run as an independent, or at least hook back up with one party or another – be it the libertarian party or the constitution party or even the green party (I wasn't being choosy, eh?) and then all of those supporters could vote for him and even if he didn't win (which he wouldn't if Ross Perot was any model of how our electoral system works) then at the very least there would be a very obvious extremely large block of Americans who agreed with his philosophy.

So I thought, right before the election, that all of use who follow the freedom agenda, could follow Ron Paul, if not to victory, at least to visibility.

Alas, it was not so. Instead of lumping all of his support towards one party, he basically said "Just don't vote for the establishment" and indicated support for "none of the above". This had the effect of scattering the vote among at least 3 other parties, completely negating any power a strong single block vote could have had.

I mean, imagine election night, and the polls are reporting HUGE percentages for the Libertarian Party. I mean, upwards of 20%, if you factor in all of the people who would have voted for Ron Paul, including write-ins etc. Image if he had thrown his support to the Libertarian Party. Even though it would not have won, it still would have garnered enough interest to be more of a real force.

Instead, he scattered our vote to the winds, told the American people that we needed more "education" on freedom, and started the Campaign For Liberty. Which if you ask me has been pretty ineffective in most ways.

One thing that bugs me about these purer libertarians, they love talking about liberty, but they have less stomach for changing America right now, so we can actually possibly live in some liberty in our lifetimes.

We had to wait for the Tea Party to have a movement which would actually drive us closer to liberty. In the meantime, Obama and his ilk have been wrecking America with pure abandon. Maybe if a major voting block had blunted Obama's supposed supremacy, then maybe things wouldn't be as bad as they are now.

Who knows. But I still think Ron Paul should have supported us after we supported him. In the end, I personally feel that he didn't have the courage to leave his party for the sake of liberty.

I know that if I were in his shoes, I would have.

Female Supremacists

I am so tired of the incessant male bashing in our current culture.

Men are people too, you know.

I can't consume any mass media whatsoever without some woman opining about how horrible men are. I can't watch a commercial without some man acting like an idiot. I can't go through a bookstore and pass a display with a book titled "Porn For Women" which had photos of men actually performing domestic tasks

I mean, this is AS bad as anti-white racism, which seems to be just as prevalent. When Holder decided not to prosecute anti-white racism, the stance from the administration is pretty clear: racism against whites is just fine.

It's the same as sexism against males. How is portraying men as idiots affecting how boys and men view themselves in society? With self-loathing?

I remember when my kids used to take gymnastics class. I have two boys, and they were in the minority in that class. As a dad there, I was also in the minority watching them bounce on the trampoline etc. I still remember the looks of derision as I walked into that estrogen filled room. Some of the women were fine, but the vast majority of the women there took the opportunity to denigrate their husbands as much as they possibly could. It was almost like a sport or a game, who had the worst husband, each regaling the other with stories of how their husbands were so hopeless, how they couldn't pitch in on the housework, how they doubted their fidelity when they were working late etc etc.

Some of the "offenses" that they described seemed pretty bizarre to me. One complained that her husband kept getting her these thoughtful gifts, and surmised that he was probably having an affair, even though he had been like that most of the relationship. Another complained that her husband had bought her a dress, and she told him that it was really nice, but then shared with the women that she was going to take it right back. Another said that he was so tired when he got home that he could barely do his share of the housework, even though it was fairly obvious that she was a full time housewife and would probably have ample time to do all of the housework and get mani/pedi's at her husband's expense.

There was little to no thought about what the husbands needed to do in order to support the family to the extent that these women would have the freedom to bitch about their husbands. It reminded me a bit of Bush telling the Iraqi people who were protesting an American summit that at least they had the right to protest now, which they never had before.

I don't know what more to say about the matter, other than to give you this thought. In most relationships, people think that there are only two parties, when in reality there are three: each individual, and the relationship. Think of the relationship as an entity of its own. Both individuals need to continue to nourish the relationship, otherwise it will die. It will die if one or the other, or both stop supporting the relationship. Too often, people believe that a relationship can survive if one party just makes up for the effort of the lacking partner. That never works, in the end the relationship will suffer and die.

Mass Media's Obituary

The press is dead. Long live the people.

One of the most interesting things to come out of the last election is that the fiction of the press being objective was finally very very obvious to everyone. I mean for the longest time, most of the press actually took great pains to try and fool us into thinking that they were objective – that they were actually reporting the facts, and that it was up to us to decide upon how to think about the issue. Ever since socialism crept stealthily into our schools, especially our journalism schools, it's been much more about saving the world than reporting the facts. It happened somewhere in the 60's, I'm thinking.

Anyways, with the catapulting of the ideal liberal candidate, Barack Hussein Obama onto the scene, the press pretty much completely gave up the fiction. I mean, those of us in the know, those of us who haven't drunk the Kool-Aid of either side, we have always been able to easily see all of the biases in the press. The election of 2008, however, basically laid it all bare – with naked support of this supposed "post-racial", "post-partisan", "post-national" candidate. The thrill was being felt up everyone's (not just Chris Matthew's) leg. However, not only did they give up all pretension of objectivity, they also latched on to the Obama "bull market" the unbelievably ridiculous notion that we had entered some new liberal democratic wave, spearheaded by our savior, Barack Hussein Obama. Like the long Republican boom before it, these people really thought that conservatives and libertarians were going to be completely vanquished. I remember all of these articles being written about the end of the conservative movement, that we are "all socialists now" etc. The euphoria from the elite and the press was incredible. This is when I realized it was time to hit the bunker, since I was afraid for the future of my country – and that this was finally the end of the grand American experiment.

How quickly things change. Turns out that what we were seeing was a minor deviation. The American people were sick of the same old from both parties and just wanted anyone but Bush and Bush style politics, which since most people really are closet libertarians, they could no longer stomach. That's what drove Obama into office – as usual it was voting against the lesser of two evils instead of voting for the right candidate.

The press, however, was in deep trouble. They had hitched their horses to the Obama bandwagon, and it was heading off the cliff. Most of them, being narcissistic ideologues, denied that there was a problem and even in the waning days, still tried to support the Savior with long winded diatribes on how Obama should "deal with" the tea party movement.

So, now that everyone's political leanings are out in the open to everyone to see, it makes it a lot easier to simply dismiss most of the mainstream media as being way out of touch with the people of this country.

And this is why the internet is so great. I'll take a blogger who sprinkles his political online rants with personal stories over a blowhard editor or writer for any major mainstream news source any day. At least I know exactly where that blogger stands on every issue. Well I guess I also know now where that editor and writer stand now too.

Firmly in Obama's camp.

Michael Moore, And Other People I Intensely Dislike

I was going to focus solely on Michael Moore in this section, but since I started writing this book, there have been so many new people that I've had to add to the list, that I figured I should at least honor them all:

Michael Moore

An oldie, but a goodie. Disguising himself as a documentary filmmaker, he makes full on propaganda for the left. His stuff looks like reality, but it is 90% fiction. He especially got my goat when he made "Sicko" making the Canadian health care system sound so wonderful, which it isn't – take it from someone who has experienced it first hand for the first 35 years of my life.

James Carville

First of all Democratic "strategists" – this guy is so annoying in so many ways – he is just an in-your-face socialist/elitist who believes that everything has to be his way or the highway. Plus, I can't stand the sound of his voice.

James Cameron

See Avatar Sucked. This guy takes the hoary old failed policies of the past, packages them up in pretty computer generated paper, then feeds them to us for 2.5 hours at a time in movie theaters and on DVD in fabulous 3D. The arrogance of this guy knows no bounds. He isn't really even a very good storyteller, if you ask me. But yet, people get sucked in by this guy.

Paul Krugman

This guy is incredible. Normally, economists are pro-business, it really part of the whole idea that if you are an economist, then you are most likely pro-business and pro-free enterprise and pro-private property. I thought that it was one of the requirements of the job: you talk and think about economics all day long, you understand that the best market is a free market. Not this guy. I think the Nobel Prize team went out of their way to find a leftist, market hating economist. I think they are rarer than real gold teeth nowadays. We all know how socialist the Nobel Prize team is, I mean they gave Obama a peace prize and he hadn't done anything yet. So with Krugman, they must have literally scoured the earth to find this guy. Anyways, he now writes for the New York Times (of course) and his diatribes go from mildly fanatical to literally insane. He hitched his wagon to Obama and is, the that dude in Doctor Strangelove, riding the nuke all the way down to the target.

There's plenty of lesser figures I detest as well, but these guys are at the top, mostly because they have fooled so many people with their message, and their lies just are so heinous and hurtful, and they are pretty loud mouthpieces. Luckily, most of us aren't swayed by the BS anymore.

Sulu Is Gay

Yes he is. Now why don't we just let people live their lives like they want to? Why do we have to tell other people what to do, if what they are doing doesn't affect us at all?

I have a few gay friends. They seem like normal people to me in every way, except for the fact that their "significant other" is the same sex. How does that matter to me? Not at all. Who am I to tell other people how to live their lives? Does it really matter to me if someone else wants to live their life differently from mine. Would YOU take kindly to someone telling you how to live your life? No.

So why do we waste so much time and energy on this issue? Is this all about government intervention again? Like I said before, much earlier on, when you trace problems back to their source, it's usually some sort of government intervention which is causing the issue:

1. Tax benefits: governments give tax benefits to married, heterosexual couples. Why is anyone getting a better deal than anyone else simply due to the fact that they are married? I think everyone should get the exact same deal, no matter what – low to no taxes for everyone. Yes, it IS possible.

2. Rights: when someone's significant other is on their deathbed, or in hospital for any reason, why can't the closest person in the world to them be there at their side, and have

power of attorney etc. In fact we already have laws which deal with all of these issues. Why do we need to make things any more complicated?

3. Immigration: right now, people can marry someone to keep them in the country, or marry someone outside the country and bring them in on a spousal VISA. This is not currently available for gay couples. See my nugget on immigration – the state shouldn't make it so Goddamn hard to get into this country. For most people, and for the USA, it's a win-win.

It's funny. I don't understand how we have the right at all to let other people live their lives the way they see fit. Unless someone is ending up with more of my money in their pocket because they are gay, or petitioned the government to fund some education program to teach tolerance or whatever, we should let people live their lives the way they like. But when it comes down to the government intruding into my life for the sake of someone else's, that's where I draw the line. So sure go be gay, marry whoever you like. But don't expect me to subsidize anything you do, no matter what it is.

I have enough to pay for as it is.

As do you.

Economic Lies

Obama claims that the economy is turning around. That's a lie. The economy is getting worse if anything. There are so many lies, damn lies and statistics out there, it's hard to tell what's real.

For example, I read today that the unemployment rate was 10.1%. Of course it will not be that when you are reading this, but who know it may be that, or even higher, if we keep going in the direction our Emperor is taking us in. This is a number I got off the Gallup organization website. An organization which is supposedly non-partisan. Let's take that as an assumption then shall we? So they poll a selection of Americans, then extrapolate to get that number. Additionally, in the same article, they report a whopping 18% underemployment. Do you ever hear that number thrown around? No you don't but it's important. Underemployment represents the number of people who used to have full time jobs but now are "enjoying" part time labor because they cannot get full time employment. Think the office worker who is now flipping burgers at Mickey D's, and just lost his house because he couldn't afford the mortgage, but is at least paying for food for his family. Nearly 20% of people out there are not in the same kind of full time employment they were in. And we are not talking people who moved from being office workers to high-priced hourly consultants. No these are people who used to have a regular 9-5 job, with probably full health benefits etc, who are now scrounging for whatever they can get in order to survive.

Add those two numbers together and you get nearly 30%. Nearly 30% of American's have lost the jobs they had. And it's probably pretty likely that those jobs are gone for good.

Now a 10% unemployment rate is optimistic. That's an average across the country. If you look at some areas, the actual rate of unemployment in some places is double that, or say 20%. In some areas, like Detroit, its 30% plus! Factor in corresponding underemployment numbers, say 28% and 38%, then in the worst off places in the country, we've lost 68% of the jobs we've had.

Nearly 70% job loss. I don't think things have been that bad since the Great Depression. Last I checked, since Obama's Stimulus bill, we've lost over 25,000,000 jobs. Most of which are never to return.

At 30% unemployment, that's 30% of the population receiving some kind of government assistance.

So the libertarian in me says: ok fine. What if these people simply started their own businesses? So what if there are no jobs – they can create their own. Well, you get slapped down there are well. There are licenses, fees, taxes, which are now skyrocketing by the way, since local governments are also running out of money. You have a downtrodden population, who get slammed down at every turn, not even able to pull themselves out of the mess the Bobama Depression has created.

Quite often, you hear Obama and the Democrats opine that the reason the economy is in such a state is because "businesses aren't stepping up". They are not creating jobs at the behest of the Obama administration. Well, it's almost like these people don't understand even the rudiments of economics. And if they don't understand even the rudiments, how can they be expected to make any moves which can improve the economy?

So, if anything, it will get worse before it gets better. And sometimes I think that's exactly what they want: the more oppressed we are, the more we are focused on pure survival, like they are in Canada, the UK, Europe, and the rest of the socialist world, the less of a chance we have to actually rise up and do something about it.

But we will surprise them in the end.

One Term President

The other day there was a CNN poll which asked, "Do you think Obama should only be a one-term president". Drudge reported it as a "Shock Poll: Most think Obama should be a one term president." I don't know about you but I don't see it as all that shocking.

In Obama's first year, he's gone from one of the highest approval ratings to one of the lowest. The only thing he has done is taken more money out of our wallets and reduced our freedoms. He has spent a ton of our money and we have gotten nothing in return: unemployment is still high, the recession is still driving people out of jobs, and ObamaCare, which will irreparably damage both the finances and the culture of our country..

Personally, I don't think that Obama feels that he needs to be more than a one term president. Since he does not believe in American exceptionalism, then being the President of the US is simply a stepping stone to something much greater, perhaps a new position, like President Of The World, specifically developed for the wonderfulness which is our lord and savior.

Don't you think? I mean look at all the international posturing during the campaign. The "Citizen of the World" comment that he made at that speech in Berlin. I mean, have you ever, ever seen a mere politician, no matter the stripe, foster such adulation? It was literally an incredible moment, where one could wonder about the future of the human race when so many of its members simply shelve their reason and submit to mob-love.

In that adulation, both in Berlin and in the scenes after it, the millions who descended upon DC for his inauguration, the free pass everyone seemed to give this guy, it was literally astonishing. Its little wonder someone like Hitler could come to power and cause all of the pain and suffering and death that he did, if the human race really has not progressed beyond that.

That is what I saw: sure Obama is a megalomaniac with an ego the size of Jupiter, but the human race let it happen. In all that sea of humanity, how many of those people actually thought to themselves "Why am I here? Why are all these people here? And what really makes this guy so special?" How many of those millions thought that before the election. This was like a mass hallucination. And if we are susceptible to that, what of the human race's future?

But I digress. This nugget is on Obama as a one term president. With the disdain that he treats America and Americans, I would think that it's not really shocking to anyone that he has set his sights on something higher – well at least he thinks its higher – that the presidency of the most powerful country in the world. Funny though, considering that he wants so desperately to destroy that power, why would anyone want him? He got this country in a beaten state, and instead of healing it, he kicked it even harder. And he continues to kick it, and will keep kicking it, until he is voted out of office in 2012.

But he'll probably say, at that time, oh well, and move up the ladder to the next role, which is only higher since he's brought America down to a level below.

There Is Hope

But there is only one hope. And that hope it to forget party affiliation. No point in getting a 3rd party in power, its never going to happen. We need to kick out the DNRs in Congress and install some RNDs (like Ron Paul) who believe in what we believe in.

I call that "The Freedom Agenda", so that I don't scare people away from it, since really at its core its libertarian, as I believe most people are anyways.

Third parties are a great idea. I love third parties (hell, I even love 4th, 5th and 6th parties). I've voted for third parties in the past. The only issue is that our system has been so perverted by the R and Ds in this world that everything is pretty much carved up between these two parties. There is literally no wiggle room between the two for any third party to grow and flourish. I know, I know, there are many of you who still hope against hope that there could be a third party someday, I just think it's no longer possible. The R and D cabal has carved things up so completely that there is no way I can see that any party beyond these two can ever have any power. And thanks to Ron Paul, to left us at the altar and didn't throw all of his weight in one direction, those winds are even more scattered.

So there is only one solution. Infiltrate both R and D (start with R since they are suffering from the sting of defeat and are currently more in line with wanting to kick the bums out – until of course they get back into power) and infect both parties and party members with the Freedom Agenda. This is almost exactly what the Tea Party is doing. And they are remaining, for the most part, completely focused on economic issues. Remember "It's the economy, stupid" – well "now, more than ever" (man I hate that phrase) it IS the ECONOMY, stupid.

If the Tea Party were to infect BOTH the R and D with the Freedom Agenda, then maybe we'll see some real change.

You see, we libertarians have something we call the Free State Project, happening way up in New Hampshire. A bunch of libertarians and other freedom loving people are trying to set up a libertarian haven up there, and while that idea is swell, and it sounds like a great place to move to – I'm more into infecting the entire country with libertarian ideals, and helping it spread far and wide.

Many "serious" libertarians detest people like Sarah Palin, or others of that ilk, who can only take us part way towards a more libertarian future. I say, ANY steps towards more freedom should be welcomed. If there is any way in which we could use the populism of someone like Sarah Palin to push the message of the Freedom Agenda, I say "You Betcha".

Spread the Capitalism

You know, I just got back from a big meeting, where I sat in a room with a lot of poor , struggling entrepreneurs and listened to a small number of people who each have more money in their bank accounts right now than I will ever have in my lifetime, and I had to pay for the privilege of doing it.

Man, did it ever piss me off. For the longest time, those who have money through luck or skill have been lording it over those who don't for a really long time. Now this nugget may feel a bit contrary to the others which have so far exalted capitalism, but hear me out.

Some of the richest people in the world currently have so much money, they will never be able to spend in in their lifetimes, and probably not in their children's, or their children's lifetimes, for multiple generations. People like the one on the Forbes 400 list (see nugget 7) have so much, yet they hold back from funding new ideas and other entrepreneurs who can take their place. At the bottom of it all, do they really fear that someone else will come along be do better than themselves?

OF COURSE they will. Everyone's time on this planet if finite, unless of course they do figure out how to extend our lifetimes (I wish), everyone's time will end.

I often wonder why you hardly ever hear about these multi-billionaires funding small innovative young businesses, finding younger versions of themselves, so to speak, and funding their enterprises, so that they too can taste some of the success? Why do they all tend to throw their money into saving the world?

If you ask me, there is plenty of time to save the world. Let's all save ourselves first. Let's all be financially successful in our own lives, and for those who have more than they can ever spend, stop wasting your money on causes which have no hope. Go and find a small, hot young business, help them to get to where you are today. Then they can go off and save the world.

And like I said before, the quickest way to save the world is to spread capitalism far and wide.

The Way Forward

Unite, or liberty dies.

Right now, as I'm typing this, candidates selected by the Tea Party, not the GOP establishment, have won in most places. People have woken up, and despite the best efforts of the mainstream media and the socialist/communist/liberal cabal holding this country hostage, the cause of liberty, the cause of freedom, is on the rise.

One of the first acts of the first "Tea Party infused" 112th Congress was to read the entire Constitution. Sure, it's largely a symbolic act, but it sure was interesting seeing the response from the left, which ranged from utter derision to pure hatred. It's a good start, but we need to do much more.

The biggest problem we have, if you ask me, is the general nature of the freedom movement, or of any movement which promotes less government and structure, as opposed to more. We are more into the chaotic, nonhierarchical way of doing things. Every man or woman for themselves so to speak. We eat our own dog food, not only do we want less government from the state in our lives, we want our organizations to be built the same way, with a loose, autonomous structures, where we can communicate the way we like. Basically the way the Tea Party is currently organized.

What does this mean? Well, you don't end up with a cohesive block of people agreeing on the details of the movement, you have a number of movements who are think the same way at the core, but differ on details and implementation. The major groups are:

1. The Tea Party
2. Ron Paul's Campaign For Liberty
3. The Libertarian Party

There are a number of smaller groups as well. You could argue that they all want the same thing: limited government, lower taxes, more freedom for people and by extension businesses and markets. So at some level, all of the groups are aligned. But then the squabbling starts: group A wants all or nothing, group B is more interested in education than action, group C wants more government intervention than others etc etc etc.

Problem is, when all of these groups start clamoring, they see their differences more than their similarities. And when they do that, the whole freedom agenda suffers.

I've heard it before: suggest offhand that Ron Paul and Sarah Palin join forces to spearhead a movement, people recoil in horror. (Actually, that is a bit strange as Sarah Palin was one of the possible choices for a Ron Paul running mate, if he ever got past the primaries – of course the GOP of the time would never let that happen) But at the core, they probably believe in the same thing.

So here is my plan: take all of the groups which look to promote the "freedom agenda" as I call it : limiting government, lowering and eliminating taxes, improving the environment for business, and unite them under the banner of the Tea Party, since the Tea Party itself is the most populous movement, as well as the most visible. Join the forces of the 4 groups above, help guide the Tea Party to a focused place, then infect the Republican party with the freedom agenda. Since there is no way a third party can win the way things are set up, we need to "take over" one of the existing parties and do that. The GOP is ripe for the picking right now. After this election, the Democrats, having been routed, will probably be ready to embrace some form of the freedom agenda as well.

I don't know about you, but I don't want to wait until after I'm gone to experience true liberty in this country. It's one of the main reasons I emigrated here – as did many others legally – in order experience the land of opportunity built by the founders. I want to make sure that the freedom this country was founded in comes roaring back, for myself, and my children, and their children, for many generations to come.

We have been tasked with this: let's do what we can to make it happen. And if it means that we have to join forces with some people which have a differing supporting vision, that's fine with me, as long as the core vision remains the same.

Life, Liberty, The Pursuit of Happiness.

- fiscally conservative
- socially liberal
- limited government

This is The Freedom Agenda. And the only way for us to get here from there is to fight our way back to it. We are so far removed from the vision our founders had for this country, I doubt that they would recognize it.

I take that back: if George Washington, Thomas Jefferson or Benjamin Franklin were to step out of a time machine right now, there would be many things that they would frown upon. Incredibly huge government. Extremely high taxation. Expensive escapades spilling American blood and wasting American treasure in battles we should have no stake in. Severe restriction of freedom of speech, of religion. They would say: this is not what we envisioned.

But then they would look, and get to know the American people. The American people have not changed. Most are still the incredibly hard working, enterprising, generous, helpful, gregarious people that they were all those years ago.

The soul of America has not changed.

The soul of American government has been sold to the devil, but the soul of America, the promise of this great land of opportunity and freedoms for all to seek out happiness, each in their own way, still beats in the heart of every American. It is still the same heart that founded this country, kept alive by the American people.

This is what the founders would see, and they would see hope. They would see that no matter how far America stays from the path it started on, it CAN and WILL correct itself, and return to its rightful exceptional place in the world.

And it is our job, the American people's job, to take us there. It's a tall order, with severe body blows from the government and its supporters trying to take us down from all sides, but we will prevail.

Because we know, that in the end, we are right.

Like I always say on my show, this is not a lecture, it's a conversation, so please feel free to contact me, I love connecting with people and discussing important issues: we may not always agree, but at least we are still allowed to speak:

- Email: thinkfuture@gmail.com
- IM: thinkfuture, on Yahoo! Instant Messenger
- Site: http://freedombunker.com
- Twitter: http://twitter.com/bunkerblast
- Facebook: http://facebook.com/chrisfutureshow

Hope to hear from you soon!